I'm Your Father, Boy

I'm Your Father, Boy

by EZRA E.H. GRIFFITH

I'm Your Father, Boy

Published by Hats Off Books™
610 East Delano Street, Suite 104, Tucson, Arizona 85705 U.S.A.
www.hatsoffbooks.com

Publisher's Cataloging-in-Publication Data

Griffith, Ezra E. H., 1942-
    I'm your father, boy / by Ezra Griffith.
    p. cm.
    LCCN 2004113004
    ISBN 1-58736-386-0 (hardcover)
        1-58736-421-2 (paperback)
    1. Griffith, Ezra E. H., 1942---Childhood and youth.
    2. Griffith, Vincent. 3. Fathers and sons--Barbados--
    4. African-American Biography. 5. Caribbean Studies. I. Title.

HQ755.85.G735 2004   306.874'2
                            QBI04-200440

To Marjorie, Elwin, Vincent, Marlene, Frank, and Joan. You walked the same pathways, and we shared supports that kept us all going, leaning on each other and on the everlasting arms. My debt to you all is profound and ineffaceable.

ACKNOWLEDGEMENTS

Writing about my early years has been a complex and intricate task, as most biographical ventures are wont to be. I have ruminated endlessly about it. I have also discussed it with relatives and friends: Joan Allard, Gilbert Allard, Bindley Blackman, Theodore Brooks, Elwin Griffith, Frank Griffith, Joan Eunice Griffith, Norma Griffith, Vincent Griffith, Grace Harewood, Marjorie Stephens, Euston Stewart, Marlene Stewart, Frederick Streets, and Brenda Thomas. They aided my efforts to be exact and to bring recollections into sharper focus, to correct distortions and shed more light on darkened thoughts. These relatives and friends have been gracious, thoughtful, and kind. I appreciate their generosity. I loved the repeated discussions about religion and Barbadian culture, both past and present.

My students in African-American Studies at Yale University also contributed to the development of the text, offering their commentary and pushing me to open up vistas that I sometimes wished to leave undisturbed.

Colleagues Josephine Buchanan, Jacquelyn Coleman, Betty Curran, Audrey Kerr, and Adrienne Roth reviewed the manuscript and helped me prepare it in its final form. Their advice and help were invaluable, as was their approach to esthetics.

Heather Manning and her staff at that wonderful boutique hotel in St. Lawrence Gap, Barbados also deserve my thanks. They welcomed me at key times and created the special ambience I needed to support my writing.

Véronique and Pierre Griffith were close companions on this lengthy and taxing journey. I am grateful for their interest and their sustained help.

Et Mignonne, je te remercie de tout coeur.

TABLE OF CONTENTS

INTRODUCTION

I think with delight about the early years, around the 1940s and 1950s, I spent with my father growing up in Alethaville, my childhood residence located in a Barbadian village called Station Hill, whose uniqueness has gradually disintegrated over the last half-century. This village culture is special to me, and I cannot separate my father from it. Alethaville is where I grew up, and it represents the backdrop for the relationship between him and me. When I talk about him and the West Indian island of Barbados, I am talking about me, about my persona that is grounded in the history and geography of Barbados, about me linked to a father I could never extract from that island.

I also love the country village of Road View, a place where my siblings and I spent the long school vacations together without our parents. It is there that I learned, at a distance from home, to experiment with Bajan geography and to feel more fully its culture, while simultaneously trying out temporary surrogate parents. I remain intrigued by how parents who are absent at those times can still make themselves felt so powerfully. It has to do with what has gone on between the child and parent before the separation takes place. It is as though the comfort of the parent's love and the parent-linked discipline established in the child's mind accompany the child even though the parent is not there. Confidence in the connection to parents seems to fuel the child's wish to explore space outside the parents' purview.

When in 1956 my family went to Brooklyn, New York, in a transnational move of signal proportions, the principal architect of the move was my father. This upheaval had significant impact on my life and on my interactions with him, who like the rest of the family was contending with the substantive stress of migrating up North. Barbados was not New York. But it is plainer to state that New York was not Barbados. It is also curious to me that a relationship between father and son can be so different when the cultural context, which must nurture the relationship, changes.

My father managed to consolidate a strong definition of who he was and to live fully and contentedly the process of self-definition. So this book is also about the transgenerational establishment of identity in different places and at different times, about preserving a Barbadian village history and culture about which we know so little.

I wish, too, to focus on the problem of preserving the wonderful memories of my youth that are especially important to me. Some are central to the maintenance of the relationship between my father and me; others are central to the maintenance of Barbadian images that still nurture me and my personal identity. These memories are connected to symbols and rituals, which are being diluted with the passage of time and by sociocultural change. I miss them the way I miss my father.

It is important to me to have this Bajan reunion, to write about me and my father and about our connections to Barbados. I think of the times when my father told me that he wanted to turn and say some things to his own father, whom everyone called the Boss. On those occasions, my father just wanted the Boss to see the world through youthful eyes. It, no doubt, would have helped the Boss to understand that there was another perspective to viewing the world. It was not helpful to my father when the Boss saw things only from the perspective of an aging man.

Sometimes in my words, all I'd like to do is articulate what I saw, mull it over, give form to an image that may bring a smile to my father's face. Often, it will be comforting enough just to voice my thoughts and reflect on some of those paths I've been down, put some order and clarity into what I experienced, just enjoy communicating with him. But I'd also like to tell him that he was right. Life without a father is different from living with a constant paternal presence. I miss him now.

I cannot change the fact that when I think of my father, a tropical lens, some Barbadian scene, always colors my vision. This is so even when I picture him sitting in his Brooklyn living room. I have really known him only in Barbados or in New York. But it was never the New

York of Americans. It was always a New York of homemade hot sauce, Mount Gay rum, the *Nation* newspaper, the dance or church service celebrating the island's independence. It was Bajan New York, which is changing, like everything else. I want to capture this social context that contributed so firmly to the defining of me and, ultimately, to the fashioning of the relationship with my father.

The morning my father departed New Haven, Connecticut, for the last time came faster than I wanted, and we shook hands without verbalizing the obvious. But how do you say to your father that you know you won't see him again? I couldn't bring myself to do it. Still, I should have been thankful, because Mamma's earlier passing was all so sudden, and I never did say good-bye to her. Our handshake filled one of those quietly momentous occasions that we often wish we could repeat.

This time I would accompany him to the door of the car at a more measured cadence, and even slower pace, supporting him all the way, because at dusk his vision was no longer to be trusted. I would not be mute this time. I would break the heart-rending silence.

As we reach the rear door of the car, we turn and face each other, extending our right arms in unison. The handshake is strong.

"Daddy, it's been a long journey."

"Yes, son, it has been long and also very good. But I'm tired now and I want to rest."

"I hope you have a safe trip home. I also want to thank you for everything you ever did for me."

"Well, I tried to do my best, son. I didn't always succeed, but I gave it a good shot."

"That's about as well as anybody ever does."

"You take care of yourself, son, and keep God first."

I help him bend his spine awkwardly so he can take his seat in the car, and our hands disengage one from the other. I reach out and lift his legs into the automobile, fasten his seatbelt around his thin frame, then gently close the car door. I take leave of a father I will not see again.

CHAPTER ONE

Fathers and Bosses

*Remember now thy Creator in the days of thy youth, while the evil
days come not, nor the years draw nigh ...*

Ecclesiastes 12:1

I remember the episode well. My father asked me to transmit a message to my mother. They were both busy in different parts of the house. Irritated by my father's request and angered by his imposition on my time, I strolled up to my mother and greeted her with this: "The man said ..." My father had no difficulty hearing my words, because the house we lived in was a typical Barbadian structure with internal partitions that didn't reach the ceiling—or if they did, there were always holes at the top to allow circulation of air. So my voice carried clearly to my father. He heard what he considered an undignified reference to himself.

He asked me, "Boy, were you referring to me as 'the man'?"

The question wasn't shouted or posed angrily. Yet there was something in the words that kept them hanging in the air, and I couldn't stop the hair on the back of my neck from standing up. Both he and I knew the reference was to him. But he wanted to know whether I understood that one's father could never be just a man. In that sense, grammatically speaking, it was not permissible for "man" to function as a pronoun and be used instead of the noun "father." The quiet but blistering tone in his voice made clear to me that in his house, I could not commit this sin of disrespectful reference. Not without wishing to deal with consequences I preferred not to imagine. So I replied quickly to his question with a tremulous "No" that I hoped apologized for the slight that derived from my boyhood anger, and I scampered out of his sight. However, that encounter, transitory as it was, marked for me the idea that I had a father, not just a man who resided in the house with my mother. That was the way it was in 1940s Barbados. He didn't hesitate to remind me from time to time, in his half-mocking, half-joking voice, "Boy, before you were, I am." My father was not a run-of-the-mill man.

Growing up, I had the experience from time to time that having him around was a burden, probably on occasions when I was having some disagreement with him. Those times are what I now call bumps along a road that bears witness to a relationship that lasts so very long, that goes on, as in my situation, even after he has passed away. I find myself often enough noting to a brother or sister what my father would have said or done if he were here to make his point. We laugh, too, when particular incidents recall him in a comical light. Of course, we can also grit our teeth when we hit the memorial bumps along the way.

I miss him, I miss my father. Before his death, he had warned me on several occasions that I would feel a profound loss after he'd gone. He had said this to me as he spoke of his own father who had long been dead. I often thought he used to say it as a way of inflating himself to look good in my eyes, which was, after all, no more than copying an honored tradition long established by Barbadian fathers from older generations. That is to say, Barbadian males who had fathered children liked to pretend that the business of fathering was akin to a religious duty. So they puffed themselves up, stuck out their chests, and claimed a solid place for the father's position in the family. "Boy, I's still your father!" was a plaintive claim that Barbadian sons would sometimes hear from fathers who were seeking forgiveness and reconciliation after years of ignoring their offspring. Still, my father was right. Once he'd passed on, I did miss him. I repeatedly wish I could have the chance to give up some special privilege in order to have a reunion with him, just to hear him spin one of his favorite yarns all over again, to hear him use his distinctive and argumentative pastor's tone.

"Man, that can't be right," he used to say. "The New Testament doesn't say that. And you are always trying to use that university education to distort the word of the Lord."

I'd have him back just to see him once more walking down the aisle of a church in a black cassock and three-quarter-length white surplice, holding his reading glasses clasped by both hands and staring straight ahead, singing a well-known processional hymn that he obviously knows by heart, neck always cocked slightly forward in a Griffithian style that he has made his, and his face reflecting an aura of ecclesiastical penitence. Every five or six solemn steps, he uses a white handkerchief to mop his brow and signature bald pate. Or better still, have him back so I can see him just once again walk up the pulpit steps in one of his favorite churches, then pause before he turns on the light of the lectern. The sermon hymn is over now, and he intones a short prayer asking for God's blessing on the sermon.

"May the words of my mouth and the meditation of my heart be always acceptable in thy sight, O Lord, my strength and my redeemer." The prayer is said slowly, with precision, and with heaviness of voice.

He looks around at the congregation, surveying them while cleaning his glasses with the edge of his surplice. In a voice perfectly pitched at a tenor level, unhurried, and with a British tinge, he declares his text. I have seen that tableau dozens of times. Once I started giving my own public lectures, I realized how brilliant and sharply honed my father's performance was. He could make the congregation wait for him, slow their breathing down, halt every movement until he released them by announcing the text. That was the preacher in my father. He understood the concept of performance as applied to the preacher's work.

From a son's point of view, then, fathers are fathers. Or at least to sons, they are always fathers first. Not professional men or artisan men or anything else. Just fathers. Whatever else takes their time and energy, to their offspring, fathers are not allowed to hide behind other titles. I recognize that many men may not be in agreement with me about this, and some of them may not like my saying so. Some fathers may suggest that their other accomplishments merit touting and are inherently more important than the acts of fatherhood. Their wives may also argue that the role of husband trumps all other functions. I understand well that historians of political leadership are obsessed with what presidents and prime ministers did in their official positions. But as a son, as the offspring of a father, I cannot think of him as a preacher without acknowledging that the man in the pulpit is my father.

Some people, for a multitude of reasons, do not know their fathers. But I have always known mine. He was not the kind of father to be found only in the penumbra of a family photograph, or a ne'er-do-well whom my siblings and I could ignore at will because he had no force of presence. That was not my father. He was the kind of man bystanders would easily characterize as having presence. I knew, regardless of where I was, that he was my father. In the early years, facing a terrifying schoolteacher or an angry headmaster, I remained confident that the disposition of the encounter would be fair. The final punishment always reflected the fact that they knew my father, and he would appeal vigorously if he thought I was being singled out unfairly. I was a little boy with a father, and I am struck now by the full import of that observation. In those days, no one spoke of female-headed households or dysfunctional families.

Having a father conferred distinct advantages in Barbadian society. I savored this the morning he gave me a letter addressed to my school's headmaster in which he simply stated that he had kept me home the day before. I was worried because the letter provided no explanation for my having missed a day of school. But he instructed me to transmit the missive to the headmaster. As I got out of the car hesitantly, he reassured me, saying, "I'm your father, boy." So in the scheme of things, in his Barbadian way of framing life, he outranked the headmaster and all others as he looked after my welfare.

We, the children, called him Daddy, a title that never changed even with the passing of time. I have been puzzled by this phenomenon. Who decides what children will call their fathers? I do not understand why we chose Daddy and not Father or Pops or Papa. But Daddy it was and has always been. My mother called him Vincent. When talking to us, sometimes she would refer to him as "your father," as when she sent us to him for his permission before she would let us do something. "Go ask your father," she would say. Or when irritated, she would threaten us with, "Wait 'til your father comes home." The clarity and precision of the threat always brought us into submission, because we had learned well from having the threat executed once or twice. Outsiders called my father Reverend Griffith or Rev or Reverend. Many of his Barbadian friends called him Griff and followed it with the ubiquitous "man"—as in "Griff, man." So the appellation others used depended on the nature of their relationship or the type of negotiations they were contemplating entering with him. On all official forms, I could always fill in the section requesting demographic information about my father and could do so with a full child's pride.

My father was born in 1911 and raised in Barbados, that small Caribbean country often referred to as the most easterly island in the chain that stretches from Anguilla all the way to Trinidad and Tobago, the twin-island country sitting just off the coast of Venezuela. Barbados was a British crown colony before it became independent in 1966, a coral island of about 166 square miles whose inhabitants have been accused in the past of being more British than anybody found in London.

My father's father, my grandfather whom everyone called "Boss," was the son of a white (likely Welsh) sugar plantation manager and a local woman from the parish of Saint John. The Boss's father may have even owned the plantation. The Boss was clearly an imposing man in his own right, since stories abound that portray him as someone well known in the Barbadian village communities of the Bridge Road and of Bush Hall, located in the relatively urbanized parish of Saint Michael. The Boss owned a horse and buggy, which defined him as someone with social standing. Not rich like a plantation owner. Or haughty looking like the British whites serving their King solicitously in the colonial service out in the British West Indies. Nevertheless, people would have known the Boss when he passed by in his buggy. He needed to use that horse-drawn contraption, of course, to visit the many sugar factories that depended on his engineering expertise to keep the factory machinery working. King Sugar ruled in those days and gave employment to many of the island's workers. This was long before anyone had ever mentioned tourism as a national enterprise through which large numbers of people would earn a living. The Boss worked as an engineer-foreman at D. M. Simpson and Company, making sure that the sugar factories were in perfect working condition at the beginning of each crop season. He did so for about 51 years, spanning the last part of the 1800s and the early part of the 1900s. The Boss knew a lot of women, and he courted some of them assiduously, while only marrying twice.

My father's mother was never the Boss's wife. In those days, bearing a man's child was not criterion enough to support the mother's becoming the man's spouse, regardless of what churches preached. I saw my father's mother on only one occasion. I concluded that she had just returned to Barbados after spending many years in some faraway place. My father took me to visit her, and I walked into her drawing room with the wariness that little boys have when they first enter places and encounter old people to whom they are unaccustomed. I was surprised by the absence of furniture in the room, except for a large trunk, the kind used by people who traveled to distant places by boat. Seeing the trunk and the massive empty space convinced me that she had just returned from what we called "away," some foreign land that my schoolboy books had not yet opened up to me. Also in the room was a strange man, whom I believed to be her husband and not my father's father. Many years later, I heard that my grandmother had gone off, only six months after my father's birth, to be a missionary in Africa. She must have been a woman of some fierce independence to make this decision, to take leave of her son and to go elsewhere, intending to speak to others about God's grace. I will not know whether her departure was full of joy or bitterness. But I have always wondered what she said in her private heart about the God who had blessed her with a child from a father who could not be her husband.

My father was raised by the Boss, who would have been 47 years old at the time of my father's birth in 1911, and a stepmother who was around the same age and had already given birth to eight children who eventually sought their fortune in other areas of the world. My father was, for all practical purposes, brought up in a home that almost all of the other children had left. A young girl, born in 1920, also lived in the house. She was the only offspring of one of the Boss's sons who had died at the age of 24 years, leaving a widow who quickly emigrated to settle in Philadelphia. From about 1923, the young girl therefore shared a house with my father, who was then around 12 years old, and the two adults in charge of their welfare. During the preceding decade, the Boss still had one son and one daughter under his roof who helped to dilute the Boss's attention and also contributed to the supervision of my father. But once those adult relatives left—the half brother died and the half sister migrated to New York City—the Boss and his wife had to raise my father and a granddaughter nine years younger than my father.

By dint of the girl's age, she evoked less concern from the Boss, although in those days, Bajan men always kept an eye on which man was showing interest in young females under their roofs. And the Boss was no different. However, my father had to be much more of a preoccupation for the Boss. By 1923, the Boss was about 59 years old and trying to cope with an energetic, rambunctious twelve-year-old boy. No doubt, too, the Boss was measuring this youngster against the reference point of the boy's older half siblings who had grown up, for the most part, in another generation and in another time. The Boss therefore saw the young boy as difficult. It may have been the result of the aging Boss's impatience or his irritability at being saddled with the boy by a mother who had departed overseas in anger. But to my grandfather, his young son must also have reminded him of a past liaison that even a dutiful wife could not have approved or easily forgotten. The stress in the house may alternatively have been at least created by a young boy's efforts to cope with a strict no-nonsense father and an acute longing for his own mother.

I have heard enough from other relatives and from my father himself to conclude that young Vincent was, as Barbadians used to say colloquially, "no sweetbread." This idiom communicates a certain restlessness of spirit, a precocious sense of independence that the Boss undoubtedly saw as belligerence, and that psychologists today call oppositional or defiant behavior. None of this was acceptable to the Boss, a man well accustomed to being obeyed swiftly and without question, whether at home or in the sugar factories. He had been fashioned by a Barbadian culture which in the 1920s believed firmly that the child, especially the male one, had to be bent, like a tree, while young . The most effective way of doing this was through regular applications of a whip and almost fanatical adherence to the Biblical principle that to spare the rod was to spoil the child.

Despite these difficulties between the Boss and his last child, young Vincent was encouraged to attend secondary school, which in those days required tuition payments from the parents, a sign of more than token commitment of father to son. The stories about the Boss's wielding of his cowskin whip make it clear that he and Vincent had a hard time forging a life together. The whole enterprise might have been totally disastrous if the Boss's wife, Susan, who was not Vincent's mother, had not made it her duty to protect the boy who was not her son. Susan worked hard to calm the troubled family waters, a task made more difficult by Vincent's adolescent stubbornness. When the Boss found a job for him in the administration of a sugar factory, young Vincent found justification to give up the position, an act that surely did not please the Boss. At another time, the Boss sent Vincent off to the neighboring island of Trinidad, where the Boss had relatives, with the hope that the change in environment would lead to a positive modification of Vincent's behavior. The Boss was looking for help to break his son's spirit.

By all accounts I have ever heard, the change in my father that left him appearing more settled and serious came about after two significant events. The first was his decision to court a young woman named Ermintrude Morris, a slim, reserved, and bespectacled dark-skinned lass who resided in the Station Hill area of Saint Michael's parish. She lived with an aunt because her parents had gone off, like many other Barbadians, to seek their fortune in Panama. She and Vincent were married in 1933, and the reality of having the responsibility for a young spouse made my father look to the business of finding a house in which to live. Their first of six children did not arrive until 1938, which provided some economic breathing room in the first years of the marriage. But things had to have been hard. In those years, Barbados did not offer a lot of choice for employment. This no doubt accounted for the extensive patterns of Barbadian migration to other islands like Trinidad, as well as to Panama, the United States, Canada, and Britain.

The second event was marked by his conversion to Christianity at some time in the early 1930s. It took place at the end of a weeklong revival meeting so common in the Caribbean. Toward the end of each night's service, the preacher usually invited people in attendance to step forward if they had decided to accept Jesus Christ as their personal savior. One night, my father did just that. He walked to the front of the church and made a commitment to dedicate his life to the service of Christ. This public testimony caused a stir throughout the church because the handsome, light-skinned, youngest son of the Boss was known to be something of a bon vivant. Time has long since effaced any clear examples, if they existed, of what my father did that characterized this period before he gave himself, in front of witnesses, to the Christian life. It may have been enough that he was seen as a young man who was at odds with his well-known father.

However, the religious conversion was significant, because it set him on the road to becoming a pastor, a unique form of public figure in those days. He earned his early stripes in the Christian Mission movement, a form of Pentecostal church to be found throughout the Caribbean. But in later years, he would speak in the pulpits of many different denominations, because his oratorical skills brought him numerous preaching invitations. Religion would become, too, a major factor in his life and would color his relationship with many people, including his own children. Over the years, my most memorable discussions with him would center on our differing interpretations of Biblical passages or on our views of what God expected from his followers in certain contexts.

My father went on to construct a life with his young bride that lasted in a partnership until my mother died in 1981. By then he had raised his own six children as well as a young woman who was a relative on my mother's side of the family. He made a major move when he decided in 1956, because of his own view of political events in his native island, that all of us should take up residence in New York City. Until I left for the university in 1959, I had lived in a home, both in Barbados and in New York, that was securely defined by the presence of a father and mother, except for the two-year period preceding the family's 1956 migration to New York. In that two-year gap between 1954 and 1956, my father was working in Brooklyn setting up connections that would facilitate the family's geographic transplantation from Barbados to New York. So our house was inviting and warm, and my father held court there in his own distinctive way, which was sharply defined by his experiences in Barbados. After all, by 1956 when we joined him in Brooklyn, my father was already about 45 years of age, an obviously Bajan (the popular diminutive for Barbadian) man living abroad.

My father was a vibrant participant in family discourse that often saw him trying hard to defend some position that his six children found ancient and inherently indefensible. But my mother's death in 1981 changed all this, and my father eventually returned in retirement to live in Barbados. After that, I saw him periodically on my visits to the island. We went to lunch or dinner and the occasional reception. Or I visited the church where he was the invited preacher. He frequently had an inside story to tell because he knew private information about public events. Besides, people always flock to tell their feelings to preachers. We talked, and he gave me advice about many things.

He also constantly monitored where I was in my relationship with his Savior. He thought it the duty of an attentive Barbadian father to verify incessantly whether his son was hewing to the right religious path. He never took for granted that I would conform readily to the Christian life. I do not mean the life of a religious, of a pastor or some other committed servant of the church. My father was talking about orienting my whole existence in a way that reflected the primacy of a decision to accept Christ. He had an innate suspicion of physicians in general. He thought their knowledge about the healing mission tended to make them arrogant, close to feeling that they could be independent of God. I found myself from time to time defending the notion that I had found a way to be a doctor who understood the place of a nascent humility in much of what I did. Selling it to a suspicious father wasn't easy.

I'm at the age now where I lose several friends in any given year. I've noticed the urgency of wanting to talk to some of them, particularly as I recognized that these close friends were dying. The other peculiar accompanying sensation is that it is so very difficult to bring the words out, to say something like, "I want to talk to you about this or that before it is too late." So with many of these friends, I play out the same fearfulness I had with my own father. I never did say to him that we should talk before it was too late. These experiences with my friends have made me come to terms with how much I miss my father and how many things I want to discuss with him. I often find myself holding quiet conversations with him, and he seems to catalyze my private reveries about past events, some of which don't even concern him directly. The intermingling of our lives has been potent enough to be one of the reasons for the constructing of this text.

CHAPTER TWO

The Everlasting Arms

The eternal God is thy refuge, and underneath are the everlasting arms ...

Deuteronomy 33:27

It was difficult when I said good-bye to my father at my home a few weeks before his passing. He was having a tough time then. The transitory ischemic attacks he was experiencing, those mini-strokes, must have been terrifying for him. He lost his balance a few times and fell, and he didn't even have the strength and the coordination to extend an arm to break his fall. Once, when it happened in front of me and he hit those green tiles in my kitchen, my heart almost stopped, then sped up, beating at twice its usual rate. I felt so sorry for him, so sad that I could do nothing to be helpful, to stop falls like that. He dropped like a baby, without the muscle strength or the coordination to cushion his fall. As he went down, his arms didn't reflexively go out to cushion the impact, and he couldn't roll the way athletes do when they hit the turf. He just dropped, hitting the floor with the not too heavy thud of a medium-sized sack of Bajan sweet potatoes. The sound of the fall was unfamiliar to me. It seemed harsh, and I know his old bones didn't like it. They had to be asking for better treatment and more recognition of their brittle state. Those bones wanted him to sit down and stop treating them with so little affection.

At another time when I had to help him with his shower, he just looked straight at me and with no provocation at all said, "Oh, how the mighty have fallen." The pain in his voice was palpable, and there was something piercingly relevant about the paraphrase of the famous Biblical verse. He uttered it spontaneously, as if he had thought of the expression himself. That's the way he talked. I instinctively knew that his phrasing had a biblical origin. When I checked later in his *Analytical Concordance to the Bible*, the book he had left me as a gift, I was not surprised at the verse's Old Testament origin or that it had come as a lament about the falling of Saul's mighty army as described in the Second Book of Samuel. These were quotidian themes for my father. It was clear that he derived power from his connection to God, from leaning on the strength of the everlasting arms. But the power had to be managed with an eye on humility, as the power of humans was never permanent. That is the mocking reminder provided by the progressive slide toward death. Everything returns to ashes and dust, and even the flower wilts as the sun goes down.

My father spoke the paraphrased verse from Samuel and recognized his own personal helplessness, which I witnessed without naming it. But he put my thought into words, and the pointedness of what he said coming out of the shower cut sharply into my consciousness. Hobbling with my support, unable to put one foot in front the other confidently, vanquished by age and time, this was not the vibrant father who had raised me. He used to dress when he had to go to a dinner or to church. His suits, while not ever being particularly expensive, always fit him in a way that made him look as though he had his own personal tailor. He usually looked grand, but in a muted, understated fashion that always evoked in me an association with London's bespoke tailors. Here then was I helping him with his shower and reflecting on the ephemeral nature of our ability to stand up and just clean ourselves. The capacity to handle even this basic task was circumscribed.

The indignity of his situation did not escape either him or me. We both knew that he had fallen, that his personal pride had been hit hard. But if it must happen to a father, it should be witnessed by his child, not by some outsider. Here was one time when the everlasting arms on which he depended so much were not there.

I did not say, "So, old man, where are the everlasting arms now?"

It wouldn't have gotten me anywhere because my father would have replied contentedly, "He moves in mysterious ways His wonders to perform."

I had also heard him preach often enough about Job to know that my father's reliance on the everlasting arms would not be diluted at his approaching demise. He liked too much that taunting phrase, "Oh death, where is thy sting?" My father was also accustomed to having his faith tested. And unlike me, he wasn't bothered by the uncertainty inherent in the gospel song chanted so plaintively by Sweet Honey In The Rock: "No one knows at sunrise how this day is going to end; can't no one know at sunset if the next day will be."

On another day, when he had one more mini-stroke, I felt powerless and particularly angry when I couldn't find a single colleague in New Haven who would agree to see him. They or their secretaries based the refusal on the fact that he was a new patient, and they weren't taking any new patients. I tried to explain that he wasn't just any patient, he was my father, and they all had fathers, and they should appreciate the difference. Furthermore, how was the classification system used by them to run their offices relevant to my problem? He was my father, whether he was an old or new patient. Then finally, a charming physician-friend of mine agreed to find time for him. But that physician was older than the others and knew what I was talking about. He wasn't full of himself, and my father liked him a lot because the doctor treated him like he was indeed somebody's father. The physician did warn me that my father was in effect dodging bullets, which meant that it was just a question of time before he was going to leave us for good.

The telephone call from Barbados came early one morning and announced his death in that usual hesitant tone that tells you immediately that something is amiss.

"Hello, Ezra. How are you?"

Niceties never work at early hours.

"I'm fine. And you?"

Silence. Then clearing of the throat in that self-conscious manner that is bothersome, almost irritating.

"Ah, Daddy passed away."

Brief. To the point. Then the usual discussion of travel plans and projected dates of the wake and funeral service.

During my flight home for my father's funeral, however, no one around me paid any attention to my grief. On flights from the United States to Barbados, passengers are preoccupied with living, with action, with doing things. Everybody is in perpetual motion, dragging bags here and there, making noise that often seems unnecessary. The Bajans going home after variable lengths of stay in the United States are greeting long-lost friends, talking about the latest cricket match, predicting the results of the upcoming election for the Barbados House of Assembly. The women are constantly fondling their gold bangles, which are struggling for space on the crowded wrists. The hairstyles run the gamut from pressed hair to jheri-curls, all the way to the shortened Afro and touching everything between these style markers.

The old men make their statement too, holding on to the habits they knew as youth in Barbados, dressed in coat and tie because that is how they used to be attired when getting on a plane, looking as though they come from somewhere, from families who have standards to uphold. Besides, on the flight they may meet someone they know, and they have to look as though they're still doing well and coping effectively with the onslaught of the aging process and the pressure of New York life. This is not to say that these older men can totally resist all the seduction of the culture up North. So I laughed when on a flight I recently saw an old Bajan man in his predictable suit but also sporting a black cap with "New York" inscribed on it in white lettering. He kept the cap on throughout the entire flight, breaking an old-time rule that male heads were to be covered only in the outdoors. After all, times have changed for everybody, I noted quietly to myself.

Of course, there are the young men, the young Turks, the cool cats, those who in a long-ago generation would have been called "sagaboys." There was a time we could distinguish clearly between those who still lived in Barbados and those who were living outside the island. But that distinction is now harder to make from just looking at them. The local chaps have latched on to the foreign styles with the intensity of a fielder in slips holding on to his first catch in a test cricket match. The latest I witnessed was a tall, slim young man wearing a red T-shirt with "Girbaud" marked on the back and a matching red cap with "Marithé Girbaud" embroidered on it. The pants were pronouncedly baggy and reaching just past the knee, which naturally accentuated his thin legs stuck into heavy dark boots. Those boots were a contradiction, especially because in the tropics they should only be worn by laborers cutting canes or repairing the roads, people who need the protection of such heavy footwear. The young traveler was oblivious to the stylistic impact of his work boots, and he saw no contradiction there at all. I resisted the urge to ask him if he'd actually been in Paris, and, if not, where he'd picked up the clothes designed by Marithé and François Girbaud. But I realized that I had recently met a Bajan in front of Paris's Notre Dame Cathedral hawking art to tourists. So the youngsters are getting around and using this newfound globalization as a stimulus to conflate the styles and to look as though they're from everywhere, not just a small Caribbean island like Barbados. This is the life they take back home on the flights.

Enterprising parents make even the little children participate in this display of conspicuous consumption. The boys are decked out in their pants and shirts that often have a label on the outside so the bystander can read it. And in the summer, no boy is wearing short pants, as my generation had to do until parents thought we were getting to be a "big boy" and, in some cases, a man. The little girls, too, are ablaze in color. The barrettes affixed to neatly arranged plaits are no longer a simple white. Multiplicity of color is the order of the day, to be surpassed only by the variability in shape or form of the barrette. The energy expended on the preparation of these little girls to face the traveling public reflects the vivaciousness of the group going home to Barbados.

Vibrancy and energy appear in the faces of even the non-Barbadians going on vacation, with their tennis racquets in the Wilson and Dunlop bags and their eyes begging for some sun and rest from the grind up North. These non-Bajans are looking forward to a promise made to them that the sun will shimmer wonderfully on sea clear enough to permit seeing the sand at the bottom of the water, and the coral beach will stretch for miles. Furthermore, the beach will not be tinged a dark gray because of its volcanic origin. No volcanoes on Barbados.

In the midst of this liveliness observed on airplanes going from the North to the Caribbean islands, there is always somebody contemplating death, heading home to the inevitable funeral. And while on several occasions I have met friends who mentioned that they were en route to some interment of a loved one, I have never stopped and asked them what the experience really felt like. It was a disagreeable trip to me. Not that one really expects the whole world to stop because one is grieving. But on the other hand, encountering death up close puts living into perspective, and it is hard to be weighing one's own vulnerability and, for example, planning a party at the same time. With death on my mind, everything else seemed so pointless, and I had no energy to participate in what seemed like frivolous celebrating. Indeed, it was the only time I would be on my way home to Barbados and not in a celebratory mood.

I sat there thinking about my father and the upcoming funeral, while the life around me pulsated. Airlines should develop a special section for the bereaved or for those preoccupied with private thoughts who don't want to bother with the noise and the bad jokes and the travelers fighting over space in the overhead compartment.

I wanted him so badly to be silent, that man with the obvious Haitian accent. No space was available in the compartment just above his seat, which in his mind became the basis of a legal brief that he proceeded to deliver orally. He insisted to the stewardess that he had a right to have the use of the space above his head. She gently acknowledged that as a general principle, he was right. However, it should have been obvious to him that on a very crowded plane flying toward the Caribbean, no stewardess could enforce rules in a context plainly made to resist disciplined regulations. As any Bajan could have told the Haitian, he wasn't looking for a quarrel, he was spoiling for a fight.

His obviously Barbadian wife was imploring him, in as strident a voice as she felt she could muster in such a public place, simply to put his bag in the other available space, the one not directly above his seat, and come and sit down quietly like somebody who had common sense. The more she begged him, the more he insisted on this right of his, with a tone that suggested he was righteously correct, according to some international convention or other.

"Alix, put yuh bag pun de udder side and come and sit down, nuh," she asked as fervently as she could.

"But I have ze right to ze space above my seat," he replied in his Franco-Caribbean style.

"You cyan see dat nuhbody en listening to you?"

"But zis space belongs to me."

"Man, sit down, nuh," was her final entreaty as she tried in vain to calm him down.

I wanted to tell him that he was interfering with my own reveries. Would he therefore be just mercifully quiet? Then I remembered that my father had been exquisitely sensitive about the business of defending his rights. But when he did it in public—in front of people, as he used to say—it had to be worth the noise and the "kerfuffle." He believed in a certain decorum. Struggling about the inconvenience of having to walk a few feet to put away a bag on an airline flight would not have been judged by my father to be worthwhile in the broad scheme of things.

The preparatory phase that preceded my father's funeral gave me little pleasure. Details needed to be discussed and taken care of, a service ritual set out, hymns chosen, a preacher invited, even a grave site selected. Fortunately for me, there were others willing to tackle those tasks. Even the few things I did evoked from me little enthusiasm. I went dutifully to see my father's body in the privacy reserved for close relatives of the deceased. This took place in a special room in the undertaker's chapel. In an instant, all the things I'd heard people say at funerals rushed back to me.

"Wuh he look good."

"Dey dress he up nice."

"He did look good in he parson collar."

"De undertaker din puff up he face too much, yuh know."

I oscillated back and forth between liking and hating the visit. I hadn't yet adjusted to the notion that he was dead.

His funeral service was held at the People's Cathedral in Barbados, where Pastor Holmes Williams was in charge. My father explicitly chose the People's Cathedral since he didn't want to be churched at the Anglican Cathedral in town, because the preaching would most likely not have been up to his standard. This was intended as no negative reflection on the preachers at the Cathedral. It was just that their style wasn't what he ever wanted at his funeral. What else distinguished the People's Cathedral from Saint Michael's Cathedral in his head remains of enormous interest to me. And it wasn't that the clergy in either church was particularly superior or inferior to those in the other faith. It was just that my father had a lot invested in how the clergy performed their rituals and preached the word. He thought that preaching was a central clergy function, and he found it hard to accept the reality that not every clergyman was a good preacher.

The hymns chosen for his funeral service were his favorites, like "Far Down the Ages Now." My sister Marlene sang as her solo, "Guide Me, Oh Thy Great Jehovah," which was one of the two hymns that had been sung at his wedding. Pastor Williams surprised me in his homily, because he ended it by playing a tape of one of my father's own recent sermons that he had given at the very church where we were. It was a spectacular moment. There he was lying in the casket, and his voice, strong and insistent, was filling up this enormous edifice with his pleas that we get right with God and prepare for the next life. It was a stroke of some theatrical genius to have him still there, with his preacher's diction making his points and everybody's attention riveted on him. I've been to many funerals because of all the church choirs I sang in, but I had never seen that done before. He was stretched out in the casket and still preaching a sermon to the assembled group. He was flat on his back, dead, and he was still able to prick our consciences with his living voice.

Since some Bajans believe in "duppies" and other supernatural phenomena, I wasn't surprised to notice a few of those present in the church looking around trying to make sure where the voice was coming from. Some of them started to cry because they felt he was talking directly to them, which was something I had discussed many times with my father as a distinct peculiarity of the relationship between preacher and listener. Others thought that since he was dead, he was already in a position to know a lot more about them than when he was alive, which effectively stirred up their guilt.

As I heard my father make plain in his sermon at the funeral of a very close friend, he was preoccupied with the living and what they were doing with their lives. He always made the point that the deceased are no longer alive. So what are the living doing with life and with what the dead have taught them? It remains a fundamental question to contemplate, one that I think flows from the relationship between fathers and their offspring. If, for example, the son is to make anything of the tutorial that he has endured at his father's feet, the son must confront the question, one that does not disappear even with the father's demise. Too many of us sons resent the question because our father has posed it. But why should the owner of the voice framing the question detract from its salience?

At the funeral service in the People's Cathedral, I felt a part of the congregation, a participant in a service that had multiple objectives, such as bearing witness to my father's ministry, acknowledging his contributions to the community, and, in keeping with his own beliefs, praying for the safekeeping of his soul. But once the service was finished and the group made the trip through the still busy Barbadian streets to the Westbury Cemetery for the committal, the group's mood seemed to change. The celebratory tone and the theme of thanksgiving that were evoked in the church service all evaporated as the motorcade entered Westbury. It suddenly hit me, as though I were still in my early years at Saint Giles Boys' School and about to discover some fact of life for the very first time, that the point of a funeral is to bury a dead person, to separate from the individual for good, forever and ever.

I had been to Westbury on many occasions in the past. But I had never found it as desolate as I did that afternoon. The goats that grazed there looked emaciated and hungry, with their ribs carefully and prominently outlined against their skin. They moved slowly, as though they hated to disturb the dead, never more than a couple of paces at any time. It was a goat version of Grieg's funeral march. Obviously the owners of the goats had not yet decided that the grass growing in that cemetery provided little sustenance for their animals. The goats were a part of the lugubrious atmosphere. I felt no welcome in the air, no hostility either. It was just blandly quiet, one of those places where I had to confront my own thoughts because there were no helpful distractions. And the realization sank heavily home that my father was irrevocably gone.

I was thankful for the warmth of the Westbury Cemetery that afternoon. This was the temperature to be expected on a West Indian island in January. When Mamma died in December 1981, I thought it inhumane to put her in the freezing ground in Cypress Hills out in Brooklyn. It was too cold. It is true that I'm a medical man, as my father used to say all the time, but my knowledge of science didn't stop me from imagining her shivering in that narrow thin box under the ground. I was persuaded at the time that Mamma had to be cold. I was cold. I was freezing. And I thought of the way she always used to be cold when she was alive. I knew she hated New York winters with a concerted vengeance, and there we were consigning her to that wintry earth.

There is something to be said about appointing a lawyer to represent the dead, the way we appoint counsel to speak on behalf of children. So Mamma's lawyer, having knowledge about how much she disliked the winter, could have spoken for her, objected on her behalf, and insisted we warm up the land first. I expect such legalistic rituals would wreak havoc with the whole business of burying dead people swiftly. Such practicalities have had no impact on my feelings about Mamma's burial. In fact, at her committal, I recall my father was there in a dark-blue raincoat with a wool lining that wasn't warm enough covering for him. He seemed to be shivering, with Ellis Sealy's strong arm supporting him, and the cold wind making the bottom of my father's coat swirl around his legs into a funereal knot.

I didn't feel the same way about my father's interment. The undertaker had strewn a lot of flowers and greenish plants around the casket, and the earth was brown and sandy dry, summery in my mind. Nobody wore an overcoat, of course, and the women's bare arms protruding from their stylish, short-sleeved dresses, attested to the strength of the Bajan sun.

At the graveside committal, nobody was so grief-stricken that there were threats to jump into the grave after my father. He and I laughed many times at that incredible old-time ritual we had witnessed in the cemetery. He worked there in the early days when I first understood that he earned a livelihood in other ways besides preaching, and I was a member of the cemetery choir for several years. So we swapped stories about what we saw there, and I used to tell him about how I loved singing over the grave, especially a psalm or "Abide with me, fast falls the eventide." The other choristers and I wove a spell with our wonderful voices that put the grieving women in a frenzy, especially the heavily bereaved. Our hypnotic tones moved the women from sedate crying into bawling, with those well-developed chests just heaving up and down. We choirboys had no need of hymnbooks or Psalters because funeral services generally demanded a limited singing repertory, which we knew by heart. With the notes wafting up into the palm trees of the cemetery, we would dare the women to match our singing with their sadness, and they rarely resisted our challenge. Naughty boys we were, and we knew the only thing they could do to outperform us was to jump into that grave, or at least go through the performance of threatening to do so.

It was our theater, and we would not let them capture the spotlight from us. So every Bajan once-in-a-while, a buxom woman from the country with no care for the sedateness of city women—she had to be from the country because no citified church woman would dare take us on—would look me in the eye and take a deep breath, utter an extra-strong scream, and rush forward. But she couldn't bluff me or any of the experienced boy choristers, fellows who could sing strong and right with no false notes and who had experience with crowds. We knew she was going to the edge, having already taken a clear measure of how far and fast she could go without falling over. I expect that none of them had studied in any detail the physics laws that governed locomotion, but they all instinctively knew what mass times velocity could do to them. They also counted on those male heroes whom I always suspected of enjoying putting their arms around those curvaceous waists to support the grieving women. This daring woman went to the edge, kicked a little dirt into the open grave, adjusted her wailing to the tempo of our singing, and then allowed herself to be pulled back, gently and conspicuously and effectively. Westbury Cemetery was our ground, said without any disrespect at all for the dead or their mourning families. But none of this went on at the committal of my father's body. Everybody was circumspect and properly nondramatic.

I never thought I would have felt my father's death as acutely as I did. For years, memories of him would come crashing back, especially during a church service in the midst of one of his favorite hymns or psalms, and I would stop singing and stand there, reflective. Silent. Things are better now. The feelings conjured up by his passing probably had to do with the recognition that both he and Mamma were gone, that their generation had run their course, which left their six sons and daughters jokingly asking about who was next in the family to go. This assumes some sort of logical generational sequence about dying; that is not the way the death game plays out, of course. In fact, recently one of my friends died a few months before her own elderly mother, and everybody was taken aback because it wasn't supposed to happen like that. A member of one generation doesn't usually jump in front of the preceding generation and claim a spot. When my father's six children stood around joking about who was next, trying hard to cover up the pain of our grief, none of us stepped up front or pulled rank to be considered first. Even Marjorie, whom my father helped raise, and who likes to assert her place in the family as the first on the spot because she's older than Elwin, my father's firstborn, didn't volunteer to be first.

Given our lack of certainty about who would be next, my sister Marlene suggested the best thing would be for all of us just to concentrate on making our "calling and election sure." She likes to throw out these aphorisms tinged with a religious patina. My father would also appreciate the Biblical reference and that it came from Marlene, who is the one in the family to have taken on the preacher's mantle he left. They discussed her very first sermon while he was hospitalized, a few days before he died at the Queen Elizabeth Hospital in Barbados. She made it clear that his passing marked an important spiritual turning point in her life, because it occurred around the time of her ordination to the ministry. She took the text of this first sermon from the 27th verse of Deuteronomy 33: "The eternal God is thy refuge and underneath are the everlasting arms." She said she preached on only the second part of the verse—underneath are the everlasting arms—and he agreed with her that the whole verse was too much meat for dissection in a single sermon. He had barely enough strength to sit up and preach his own sermon right there in the hospital room, as he delineated some of the points he would have made if he had been in a church's pulpit. I could see Marlene sitting there taking mental notes and filing them for some future exposition.

Years before, I had done a clinical elective in that Barbados hospital. So I knew how simple and bare the rooms were, how plain and pervasively tainted by an antiseptic smell. Still, I always loved the sunlight that entered the patients' rooms, accompanied regularly by a breeze that took advantage of the unimpeded entrance afforded by open jalousie shutters. The wind and the sunlight compensated for what the hospital lacked in technology; both the healers and the patients were connected to God's special grace.

My sister and my father talked in a hospital room about a Bible text that presaged his own impending demise. It would indeed have given him strength, even if for only a short while. He liked exploring the context of the story before setting out to explicate the meaning of words in the single verse. Then he linked the text to other stories in the Bible, which was a habit he had of demonstrating over the years his thorough assimilation of this single book. And to stir up any of his listeners who thought that they too knew the Bible well, he cited names and whole verses from memory. He was especially proud of this talent because he had used it to defend himself as glaucoma dimmed his sight. I could also grasp why that Deuteronomy verse would excite him so much. There can be no other time or place when the importance of the everlasting arms is as immediately crucial as when one anticipates the end of one's life. My father knew that his days were numbered. That was the time when his faith had to hold strong, when the belief in the sustaining arms of God had to be immutable. I wish I had been there. He would have looked at me and said that he had held fast to his faith just so that he could be confident as he stood on the threshold of encountering his Maker. That was all part of the business of making one's calling and election sure. But he had also faced me down on many occasions over the years with his claim that the surest refuge was the everlasting arms of God, particularly in the face of trial and tribulation.

In the dialogue with Marlene, my preacher sister, my father was squarely in the midst of central questions about him and his God, which we had discussed interminably over the years and which Marlene and I now have taken to dissecting from time to time. What goes on after they put us in the ground, when all the singing and praying are done and the grave diggers, some of whom my father used to supervise, have heaped the dirt so unceremoniously on the coffin? We Bajans still like that part of the ritual. We stand there and watch those men spading the earth back into the hole. Many of the men used to be barefooted, with not a smile or even a scowl on their faces. Just blank, emotionless. Merely a job, nothing personal. The small rocks would hit the coffin, and I would wonder if the dead could hear it, the peculiar noise that sounds like nothing else at any other time. Does God grade us on how hard the family cries or on how many hymns we sing around the grave?

But I return to the rocks and the dirt hitting the coffin. It seemed disrespectful, as though I were pelting rocks at my own father. Why do we do that? All the dirt thrown on the dead should have to go through a strainer, the way my mother used to pick and wash rice in the old days before she set to cooking it, to get out the "weebles." We should have done that for my father, brought together friends and family and spent days sifting through the dirt, removing anything that would make an unwelcome noise when thrown against the coffin. After all these years of carrying out the same ritual, burying the dead in the same cemetery, the ritual should have been improved, shaped up to look more considerate and humane. We solved the problem of the cold by burying my father in Barbados. But to my mind we encountered another unexpected problem: the sharpness of gravel and pebbles hitting the coffin of the defenseless dead.

It is my father's position that we shall be judged by our works seen and not seen. But many of us have performed so very badly that I am uncertain how much comfort I can take from his argument. If there is fair judging, there is going to be hell to pay. Even with maximum grace and forgiveness, I can't see many of us making it. Do those who go before us really get to put in a word for or against us? How does that get weighed in the scheme of things? If we knew the answer to that, then some of us might be vindictive enough to ask to go earlier, just so we could screw things up for someone we didn't like who was coming after us. But we won't know, which brings us back to my father's approach that required faith in a certain orderliness to the outcome, which in turn persuades us of the importance of behaving in a particular manner, or at least trying to do so.

I once told my father that one of his most disappointing sermons I ever heard focused on trying to give an explanation for a young girl's death. It was a very sad funeral, and he took on the challenge of justifying the girl's passing. It was a heroic effort, and I responded to it all with alternating frustration and anger.

"Daddy. It wasn't a very good sermon, you know."

"Why do you say that?"

"Well, you danced around the central issue."

"Which one?"

"You don't know why the girl's life was ended so early. But you kept on talking as though that was not important."

"God has his plan. The young girl could only have been taken as a part of that plan. You can't question God."

"If I can't question God, at least I can own up to my ignorance about God's actions. You keep quiet about the things you don't understand."

"I'm not running from my ignorance. I just have faith that things work out in the scheme of God's plan for us. It is your lack of faith that makes you so irritable and dubious about events like the girl's demise."

"I'm not convinced. As a preacher, you're afraid to acknowledge what you don't know about God's workings."

"You, my son, keep accentuating ignorance. I am not in competition with God. It is my faith in him that sustains my belief about whatever he does. You can't grasp that because you think you can be independent of God's plan."

Over lunch recently in New Haven, I reviewed this subject with a preacher-friend of mine who had just lost his brother to cancer. Facing death, the brother had made it clear that he was content with what God had decided. This dying brother removed all my questions with a sweep of his hand, clearing away the words that were cluttering up the scenery. He narrowed the focus to the basic subject of faith, which he employed to still his fears and resolve the other questions to come. He was in God's hands, and God would, in everyday Biblical parlance, work His purpose out. The brother was confident that his needs and God's purpose were concordant. That was, to a certain extent, what my father was trying to argue. He wouldn't accept my questions because he had his faith. Put another way, my questions were reduced in importance, at least to him, by the power of his faith. He had always liked Martin Luther King's speech about the Promised Land, especially since it confirmed the reasonableness of his hope that there was reward for the effort expended here on immediate tasks. But he liked, too, the implicit reference that the ultimate promise came from His shedding of blood and His giving of life, the supreme sacrifice that Jesus made. In my father's terms, all of the questions were worked out by his fundamental understanding that the eternal God was his refuge, and underneath were the everlasting arms.

CHAPTER THREE

Sing-Ins and Brams

*O sing unto the Lord a new song: sing unto the Lord, all
the earth. Sing unto the Lord, bless his name ...*

Psalm 96:1-2

Whenever my birthday came around, my father would call or
write to remind me that he was there when I was born and
that I first saw the Barbadian sunlight from a small house
located in a gap off the Bank Hall main road. He would tell me how he'd
gone to find Ms. Alleyne, the midwife who delivered me. My birth likely occurred in the very house the Boss finally helped him obtain. When
he and Mamma decided to marry, he went to the Boss and told him
about their plans and then sneaked in a quiet request for some financial
help. The Boss swallowed twice before replying with his usual gruff
causticity.

"You buying a horse and expect me to buy the stable?"

The help eventually came. Bajan fathers often have a change of heart
and help their children, but not until the fathers have grunted their dis-
approval and forced an obsequious demeanor on those soliciting a favor.
It is an ancient ritual that the favor must not be granted in a way that
suggests a generosity of spirit or that makes the father look soft and loving.

Doreen, Mamma's close friend, often used to say she too was there at my birth, which was her way of saying she knew me before I could formulate any words to talk back to her, to represent myself, as Bajans say. When she reminded me of this fact in a reverent tone, it was Doreen's way of arguing for special status, of claiming that she was some kind of surrogate mother to me, which was true. What she wished to ignore was that I was also obligated to a host of other mothers because of the nature of the old-time village life in Barbados. Doreen had indeed played the role of surrogate mother at times, which didn't stop my father and her from having differences much later on in New York. She had helped out Mamma and had even stood in for Mamma, taking care of my siblings and me when, for example, both parents were in Trinidad and we were still in Bank Hall. This was before we children rejoined them in 1944 in a Trinidad that offered employment linked to the war effort.

After we left Bank Hall, my father insisted that I had a duty to pay respect to and to be reverent to the people who continued to live there, since they had known me for so long. It was also because they had helped Mamma in numerous ways, at a time when she was rearing four children in conditions of minimal material comfort. Men in Barbados never asserted this sort of linkage in quite the way the women did. Men never claimed to watch me shed my navel string or even pretended that they had helped burp me after a meal.

Huntie was another of those special women. She was in a class by herself, and she was never Mrs. Hunt to me. She established her own special attachment to my second-oldest brother, which explains why she was addressed so endearingly by the abbreviation of her last name. I called her Huntie because family tradition sanctioned it. I can conjure up only a very faint picture of Huntie. On the other hand, I know the smell of her house, that scent coming from the inside of a small wooden home occupied by an old woman no longer particular in taking care of her surroundings. The air was stale and seemed to foster the growth of cobwebs, which were in turn rarely disturbed. Newspapers occupied furniture longer than would have been the case when Huntie was younger and stronger. But when I knew her, such precise orderliness was unimportant in Huntie's life. She saved her energy for saying her prayers every morning and night, for thanking the God who let her see another day of sunshine, and for appreciating little rascals like me who managed to find a minute to stop by and provide her contact with the young generation.

Mrs. Blackman lived in the house opposite ours. I went to the same elementary school later with her two sons, and her daughter also became a good friend. They all constituted a lifeline to Brathwaite's Avenue, which was one of the multiple side roads flowing off the Bank Hall main road. Mrs. Blackman was, of course, much younger than Huntie, and she had young children to keep her vibrant and busy, and a tall, lanky husband whom I never knew well.

I called Mrs. Herbert "Doreen" because I knew her before she was married. In any event, her surrogate-mother role demanded something more affectionate and less formal than a married name. She always remained associated in my mind with Bank Hall even though she lived elsewhere. She continued to visit us for years afterward and never let me forget that she sent me to lessons with Mr. Harris, a teacher who gave after-school instruction to pupils in his home on the opposite side of the Bank Hall main road.

Mr. Harris was one of those individuals who helped define the Bank Hall area. He was an elementary school teacher, a diminutive man who wore a tie and long-sleeved shirt, with bands that went around his biceps and shortened the sleeves by allowing him to blouse them so that the cuffs of the sleeves would fall smartly on his wrists. He was also at that time the only person I knew who played the violin. Mr. Harris's lessons were a part of my elementary school years, and they cemented my everlasting connection to Bank Hall.

As I became a young boy able to travel by myself, a week rarely passed by without my going past the Bank Hall area. That is because of Bank Hall's geographic and emotional centrality, despite its obvious smallness. The Bank Hall main road runs east to west for a distance of about a half-mile. It starts at the four-way junction of Hindsbury Road and the Bridge Road and stops at a four-way intersection where the Outrams used to live. But off this main road flow numerous small arteries, going both north and south and themselves intersecting with other tiny byways. I believed there were thousands of people densely packed into this circumscribed area that was quite near to Bridgetown, the capital of Barbados. Bank Hall was on a major bus route; it housed many of my close school friends, both male and female. My main buddies in the Cathedral Choir lived there, and it was home to Empire, the football club I hailed for. It was hard to do much in my early life that did not take me by that area.

At strategic points along that artery, there were women sitting by wooden trays under a streetlight selling peanuts and sugar cakes. In the early evening, they might also be offering roast corn while they fried liver hard as nails, which my buddies and I used to love to put into a penny loaf of bread to form the sweetest "cutter" ever known to cross a young boy's mouth. These days, my cosmopolitan friends talk about the delicacy of liver gently fried and still softly oozing blood. None of that has the odor of liver, which we called "harslet," fried so very hard that it took on an indescribable consistency. And the cooking smell I have so adored all these years came from the commingling of different seasonings. Friends have taught me only recently the multiple possible origins of this fried liver: from old cows, young calves, and pigs. The consensus is that I must have been eating liver from the pig, likely half-fried in a shallow frying pan and then also stewed up in a deeper iron utensil called a buckpot. Every Bajan of my generation is partial to the fried liver of his youthful environs. For me, Bank Hall or Roebuck Street was the place to get it. Forget Baxter's Road or any other place being touted by partisans from those regions.

We didn't stay long in Bank Hall after I was born. The Second World War was in full swing then, and my father moved us to Trinidad, where my sister Marlene was born in November 1944. My father took a substantive decision in making the move from Barbados to Trinidad during the war. He moved a wife, who quickly became pregnant, and four children, including Marjorie, and took a new job in a different culture at a time when Europe was in an uproar. He also temporarily severed supportive ties to relatives and friends, which caused at least a modicum of hardship. The financial opportunities presented in Trinidad resulted from the industrialization that was promoted by the war. But Trinidad may also have offered a respite for my father from something stressful in Barbados.

I still have faint recollections of stories about evil spirits, called "sukiya" (probably a term derived from French patois), capable of sucking the blood of children. My mother's words of caution made me fearful of snakes that reportedly could be found hanging from the rafters in those small Trinidadian wooden houses. I was quickly familiar with the term "Shango" and its association with religious ritual and drumming. My father loved to tell the joke about a Trinidadian shopkeeper who one day was terrorizing a female customer in his shop. The shopkeeper was, in fact, only sharpening his cutlass. But every time he passed the blade over the sharpening stone, he would intone, "Prepare ye for the coming of the Lord. Are you ready to meet your maker?" The woman decided that such an inquiry suggested the end might be near. So she started to scream. My father liked telling that joke about Trinidadian folk personalities, and I always thought it delightfully funny.

The Trinidad economic boom fueled by the war had begun to subside, and after two years, my father thought it wise to head home, to family and roots and connections and sustenance.

We returned to Barbados around January 1946 and settled in the Brittons Hill area, reached by going straight up Beckles Road, continuing up Dalkeith Hill past the church on the left, and running into Brittons Cross-Road. A right-hand turn while hugging the wall eventually leads to the second road on one's right, which is Rollins Road. The first turn is actually a dead-end, with a few imposing houses where important white people always lived. But on Rollins Road was our wonderful house, down in that cul-de-sac, with a broad porch wrapping around it, big enough for me to run a tricycle on it without fear. The house carried the name of "First Attempt," which at the time aptly fitted the circumstances of everybody in it. I could see the blue of the Caribbean Sea from that porch and could feel the winds that kept the area cool and protected from the tropical heat.

I recently went down Rollins Road looking for that house with the beautiful wraparound green porch and the imposing view. I found what I suspected was the house, and I went and introduced myself to a gracious old lady who lives there now. She had known my father, and she recalled his being a preacher. She also remembered laughingly that Mamma was pregnant when we moved there, likely with Frank, and she said she joked with Mamma that even though my father was a man of God, he still found time to make babies. That was a joke she said she had teasingly related to Mamma well over fifty years ago. My father had rented the house at that time from a gentleman who worked at Alleyne Arthur Company and managed the house for the owners, after whom the road was named. Rollins Road is no longer a cul-de-sac. But most disappointing to me was the fact that the wooden house had been redone, recast now as a structure of wood and cement blocks, and my wooden porch, my bluish-green wooden porch, is no more. The view remains spectacular, and I could see in a thoroughly unimpeded fashion all the way from that Brittons Hill site over the roofs of the houses down to the Caribbean Sea. In the yard was an abandoned limekiln that was not a part of my memory, as well as an unforgettably imposing mayflower tree with red flowers and dark brown shack-shacks, the correct name of which I have just never learned. Maybe the shack-shacks constituted the fruit of the tree. There were no longer any holes that hid crabs, which I had played with at the time, poking sticks in the holes to make them emerge just at the time I would scamper off. I never wanted to become entangled with their claws, which had seemed so enormous and threatening to me.

I was about five years old then, young enough to be terrified one afternoon returning from Bay Street Boys' School where Mr. Cuffley, a friend of my father, was headmaster. As I turned the corner into Rollins Road, I was kicking an empty can along the road when a man ordered me to stop the noise or he was going to get the police after me. I took off running through the air like tumbleweed in the windy desert. I thought the man snickered, without imagining how terror-stricken he had left me. I later came to understand that Bajan men loved to put order in their own lives by controlling children around them and instilling fear here and there. So what if the poor child even peed in his pants? I have had the idea all along that this toying with children, this perverse humiliation of them, was taught to Bajan men by the British. It was one way the local black men could redeem the leadership of their own lives, by dominating the weakest around them.

Experiencing the slickness of an older boy at school also reinforced the reality of my youthful years in Brittons Hill. One day, after classes were dismissed, I was waiting to be picked up by my father. I was in a shed where carpentry was done, and there was a lot of sawdust spread around the floor. The clever older boy created a mound of the dust, then put his ear to it and told me of the wonderful sounds he could hear emanating from the pile. He appealed to my imagination, and I put my ear to the pile, intrigued by the potential for sharing in this unusual magical happening. The boy then blew the dust in my ear and rocked back laughing. The headmaster was nearby, and I complained vociferously to him between sobs. He calmed me down and meted out no punishment to the boy, who in my mind had been transformed by then into evil incarnate. I wonder now if the headmaster had been chuckling to himself and saying that's what schools are for, to make little boys into older boys who can fend for themselves in a world peopled by both friends and tricksters. At the time, I was taken by the unfairness of having to deal with others who had the distinct advantage of size and experience. I was struck by the headmaster's unwillingness to "give me satisfaction," or mete out retributive justice. I had been made a fool of, but I recognized I had no basis on which to complain further. I did not tell my father, who was in my mind always competent and willing to represent me and take on the world. I could not have told him that I really believed sounds could emanate from a collection of sawdust lying on an ordinary schoolroom floor in Barbados. That would have let him down. Not even at five years of age could I have confessed to believing such foolishness. I did not believe it. But I was not yet beyond hoping that it could be true.

We did not stay long in Brittons Hill, because the house we moved into next, which was located in Station Hill, came rent-free. "Alethaville," the name of the house, was imprinted on a painted piece of metal and hung high up on the front of the house, just below another metallic sign shaped like a royal crest and bearing the name of the insurance company that insured the dwelling. The house belonged to Daisy Aletha Taitt, Mamma's aunt, who lived at the time in Brooklyn, New York, somewhere in the Bedford-Stuyvesant area. I didn't know Aunt Dais then, and it would be slightly more than a decade before I would meet this woman, who apparently frightened even adults with her no-nonsense manner. But there we were, living in her house, off her apparent beneficence, an act of kindness that she never let me forget in later years. Stated more precisely, it was an act of Christian charity she emphasized to me years after, one she thought my father had chosen to forget and that she enjoyed restating, the way politicians enjoy restating their achievements in an electoral campaign. Like Doreen's gift of sending me to lessons at Mr. Harris, Aunt Dais's kindness was expected to bind my father to her in a lifetime of dutiful appreciation. This is not to say that in these situations, the donor is unreasonable in her expectations. It is just that the recipient isn't always ready for the lifetime of fealty and obligation. Still, the donor's gift is real. And it is a decades-long tradition among Barbadians that those who give of their largesse keep score for a lifetime.

In the 1930s, Mamma lived in Alethaville with Aunt Dais, and with Ma and Pa Hinds, Aunt Dais's own parents. At that time, Mamma's mother and father had gone off to find their fortune in Panama. I never knew the parents of Mamma or Aunt Dais. So when we moved to Alethaville, Aunt Dais had been long gone, having rushed off to New York sometime in 1932. Her ex-policeman husband had preceded Aunt Dais to New York several years earlier and had fathered Marjorie in a liaison with a mulatto woman. This was the cause of Aunt Dais's rapid decision to head for New York. Marjorie was swiftly bundled up after being christened and sent to Barbados in the care of some woman heading home by boat. My father met the boat at the docks, collected Marjorie, and took her to Mamma. My father and mother were not yet married. Once they did get married, Marjorie was the first child in their new home, since Elwin, their own offspring, didn't arrive until 1938.

Of course, Marjorie was a full-fledged member of our household, a status I don't think she ever reached in the New York residence of Aunt Dais when Marjorie went to live with her and Mr. Taitt in May 1949. I was too young then to grasp all the nuances of the news reaching Barbados. But I certainly figured out that Majorie had a difficult time adapting to Aunt Dais's unique style, and the news cast a cloud over Alethaville that I could not penetrate. Children weren't allowed in big people's business. My father never said much either, at least not to me. But Aunt Dais and Marjorie weren't ever going to get along. Marjorie's stunning attractiveness, and what the Bajans would call her "light skin," could not enhance her status in Aunt Dais's eyes, reminding Aunt Dais at every turn of the other woman. No one ever talked about the trauma Marjorie's mother must have seen, odd woman out that she was, and no one ever explained how the mother could have been persuaded to give up her child to be raised in Alethaville.

Modern-day theorists talk about this business of breaking bonds between parents and child and give their opinions about whether it could ever be good for the child. This was a common occurrence in the Barbados of old, when parents up north sent their children to be raised in the Caribbean. Alternatively, parents back home left their children and went to make a living elsewhere, sending back the dollars or pounds regularly to relatives raising the children. That was just the way it was, a form of adaptation to the fiscal and to the other social realities of the time. So Marjorie knew Mamma as her mother and couldn't therefore easily conform to the disciplined regimen of Aunt Dais's Herkimer Street, in a Brooklyn that was new, different, and so unlike the Alethaville in which Marjorie had grown up. I would have my own taste of what these moves meant when, with my siblings, I would make the trek to Brooklyn in 1956. But in Marjorie's case, while the separation from her biologic mother could not be painful to her, because she was a mere babe in arms at the time she was taken, the reunion with a father and stepmother she never knew could only be problematic.

One could reach Alethaville by going up Station Hill, past Glendairy Prison on the right, and past the entrance to the home of the commissioner of police on the left. Then about twenty-five more yards would lead to a road on the right. You couldn't miss the turn because it was the first right after Mr. Moore's rum shop, which was housed in a wooden building likely constructed in the early 1900s. The section of the building serving as a British-version tavern was on the ground floor. The first floor had a porch that stuck out into the air without any visible means of architectural support. No one ever seemed to sit on the porch.

Our gap, which had no name then, was a little more than a hundred yards in length and wide enough to accommodate an Austin motor car, something rarely asked of it because a car then wasn't an option for many people. It was a gap, not a real road, and not covered with tar and flattened out so it was smooth. It had marl and big rocks and small stones that caused the gap to be particularly uneven. When it was dry, the gap was dusty. When it rained, there were puddles and slippery stones to be avoided. People who lived there knew their gap intimately, understood where to guide their bicycles or their Sunday white shoes to avoid incidents and accidents. And to taunt outsiders, each end of the gap had a slight promontory that was steep enough and uneven enough to make cyclists or drivers hesitate. The hesitancy could be long enough to make the driver's car engine stall, because in slowing up, he hadn't pushed in the clutch fast enough and downshifted to a lower gear. Similarly, the unsuspecting cyclist could turn into the gap without the requisite speed, brake to avoid a rock, and then be unable to ride over the slight incline. This could require a precipitous dismount that often ended with the cyclist hurriedly trying to avoid falling in front of amused children.

Later on, after I had left Station Hill, the gap was given the unnecessarily grandiose name of Second Avenue, Goddings Road. It is true that modernization has rejected the old-time way of establishing coordinates. Progress dictated change, but it made little practical sense because no one ever got lost up in Station Hill. You couldn't lose your bearings while trying to find Alethaville. Going up the hill, you didn't have to pay attention until you reached the prison. And if you saw District A Police Station, then you had gone too far. Coming down the hill from the direction of the country, you could ask any bus conductor to let you know when you had reached Savannah Road on your right, which was the first turn before the police station. Once the bus going down to Bridgetown reached the prison, you had bypassed the gap. Any schoolboy could find us. If you were walking or on a bicycle, then it was child's play. All you had to do was to stop any adult, say good morning or good afternoon as required by the village culture, and ask about Alethaville where the Griffiths lived or, more specifically, for Reverend Griffith.

Alethaville was located practically at a point equidistant from the beginning of the gap, where Mrs. Cobham resided, and the end, where the canes of the neighboring Waterford Plantation started. That latter point was the area we called the Bottom. The gap dipped down into a sort of valley, along which ran a road that was perpendicular to our gap and is now called Goddings Road. Today, at the intersection of that road and the gap, down in the Bottom, you can find the Lashleys. The sons had played with me at just about any game permitted by the geographic terrain and space: pitching marbles; playing cricket, football, cowboy and crook, and table tennis; foot races; and even high-jumping, made possible by stringing a rope between any two objects that could take the pressure.

Alethaville was a house made of wood and cement, or what we used to call a wall house, which wasn't the same thing as the bungalows that they were building up in Kingston Terrace that were made all of wall.

Outsiders will, of course, ask what "wall" was, as though it might be something like stone or brick or a cement block. "Wall" described all of those entities but relied more on establishing the contrast with wood. If you had a wall house or a house that was partly wall, it meant you were making progress, moving up from the plain wood chattel house. As a result, Alethaville's partly wall status gave it a certain standing in the village. A small garden in the front abutted the gap. Since no town or country-planning agency existed in those days, no setback from the public road was required. In the back of the house was enough land for trees to grow and a vegetable garden to prosper. Marlene, more attuned to agriculture than I, says that we had coconut trees, tomato vines, lime trees, and a papaw tree back there.

Looking at the house from the road, on the right was the Holder family, with Mamma's goddaughter. On the left was the Brathwaite family house, separated from us by a garage for our family car, room for chickens and two stalls for pigs, and a yard for our football and cricket games. Mamma also eked out space on that side for a confined rectangle of rocks, on which she dried our clothes in the "boiling hot sun," as the village women termed it.

The house itself was not big, although by yesterday's standards, it was comfortable. The drawing room was a rectangular space with a front door flush in its middle and opening on to the gap. Two windows looked to the front, and a side window permitted Mamma to chat with visitors without having to get properly dressed to receive them, since they stayed out and she stayed in. A second side window, which looked on to our yard, enabled me to play all kinds of games in which I practically dived through the window in either direction without getting hurt. The two front windows were strategic observation posts, used at key moments of the day or night to watch both the mundane and the unusual. From those windows, I could tell in the light of day who had gone to work, who was fetching water from the standpipe on the main road, and who was visiting the neighbors at any point in the gap. They also allowed physiological analysis of every young woman's walk, both from behind and in front. The analysis was done without audible comment, as every little boy had to know when not to give voice to his thoughts around adults and especially fathers. Those disciplinarian fathers hid for a long time the fact that they were observant and appreciated the young women's gait. The windows of Alethaville witnessed many a bamsie—a polite Bajan reference to the female derriére—some rolling in a thoughtful but prosaic way and others grinding hurriedly and creatively as the owner moved about purposefully on some clearly defined errand.

It did not seem an unusual day. But the morning those two dogs started mating right in front of Alethaville, it was hotter and stickier than usual. A group of onlookers like myself started pointing fingers and laughing. It may have been that too many children were in the group surrounding the dogs. My father got enraged and took off the heavy leather belt he wore. Then he tore into those two dogs, expecting that the pain of his lashes would force the dogs to separate. The chemistry and physics of canine fornication kept the dogs stuck together, to the delight of the youngsters in the crowd. My father's frustration increased, since he had taken on a task that should have been quickly concluded so that he could walk off looking very much the protector of village values. Instead, he provided a theatrical experience for everyone around, with Alethaville as the scenic background.

The poor dogs took a licking that day, since nature would not be short-circuited by the morality of mere men, especially preachers like my father. The dogs absorbed every blow until biology had run its course, and my father, spent from the exertion on a hot Bajan morning, sought refuge inside. I never saw those dogs again. They had understood that Alethaville was not a preferred site for their extravagant and impulsive rendezvous. They could have preferably met near the marlhole behind Miss Garner's house, away from prying eyes, and could have avoided that encounter with the Reverend.

Of course, his attempt to protect the morals of our community in the gap had a slight ring of falseness to it. After all, even little boys like me knew what sex was all about, and whether or not my father and his church colleagues wished it, sex was a powerful preoccupation of those living in Bajan villages.

It is amusing and also curious that I was recently sitting at a restaurant in Barbados having dinner, preoccupied with putting some hot sauce on two fried flying fish. On the beach, located squarely in front of the restaurant, two dogs started to romp. Then one of them got carried away by his hormones and started to mount his companion, in full view of an audience who tittered and giggled. Eventually, the manager of the restaurant went on to the beach with a pail of water and threw it on the dogs. They scampered away in what I would call canine embarrassment. But I couldn't understand why the manager felt somehow duty-bound to interrupt the dogs. For me, the incident remains a symbol of the paradox to be seen in Barbados, witness to the long tension between religion and the other secular activities of a community so pervaded by calypso, teenage pregnancy, and repeated references to carnival-type celebrations.

Only a few of us saw this puritanical side of my father in those early years. But it emerged again in all its holiness when a particular woman, whom our whole family adored, would come to use our telephone, since we were the rare family in the village with this contraption for communicating with others. She was a delightfully sensuous lady, full of life and zest, with a heart of gold for the children around her. She was, like many women of the time, practical in her view of life and open about it. She maintained a relationship with someone who provided for her and visited often and openly. The woman had a man, we used to say as a routine matter of fact with no judgment intended. I liked the man, especially because he liked children and found it easy to engage them in conversation. While not flaunting the relationship, the woman knew it was pointless to try to hide it. Secrecy in the village was not a viable option. Bright enterprising boys in the gap knew by heart the car number of any vehicle daring to penetrate into the area more than twice in any week.

The fact that the man had a wife created a moral problem for the Reverend and offended his sense of what was right. So he instructed Mamma not to receive the woman when he was at home. Mamma told the woman, and the flouncingly lively lady made the adjustment without a problem. She came to see us when the Reverend was at work. The women understood those things and simplified life before a mountain was made out of a molehill. A smile too passed between the woman and Mamma, making it clear that the Reverend was just showing off. After all, people had to make a way and live a life, and many of the Reverend's male friends, including some of his pastor buddies, were behaving worse than the woman. That's why the woman and my mother smiled knowingly and let the matter drop. There was no need to turn the issue into a major philosophical debate. But the point was obviously made that my father was not criticizing or refusing to have social contact with his many male friends who everybody knew were having dalliances with women not their wives.

Years later, the woman showed up at Mamma's funeral in Brooklyn and reminded me who she was and offered me a shoulder to cry on. But I had long since picked her out of the crowd. Even with age, she still had that verve and a smile that she could flash captivatingly. She was the kind of woman whom I wished in my youth I had been old enough to talk to and ask about how she made the decisions in her life. She had knowledge of the rules, and she broke them all in a way that still endeared her to those who really knew her. She was always there to be helpful to other villagers who needed a hand. At the same time, she would defend herself quite effectively if you interfered with her or those she loved. It was a pity that the preacher side of my father prevented him from being more amiable with her. But that was a time when his religion got in the way of sympathy and prevented him from being as accepting as Mamma was.

My mother's sensitivity to the needs of women gained her a reputation in the gap. Another woman had decided to give a birthday present to a younger man she was dating. She bought the gift but then had no place to hide it until she could give it to the intended recipient, because she couldn't maintain absolute privacy where she lived. So quite naturally, she asked Mamma to keep it for her, knowing Mamma to be discreet and understanding in those things.

One morning, a neighbor consulted Mamma with a perplexing question. The woman had a husband with an annoying streak of irritability that led him at times to throw plates and an occasional glass into their yard, because in those days, angry Bajan men got back at their spouses by breaking things of which their wives were proud. Just at the backdoor of our house, the neighbor commenced her consultation with Mamma.

"Mrs. Griff, I accidentally come 'cross this money my husband did trying to hide from me. You tink I should gi' it back to he?"

Mamma thought for a very short while and then said, "Your husband tell you he lost something?"

The elegant simplicity of the interpretation shattered the silence. The woman knew instinctively that returning the money was certain to provoke a confrontation with her husband because he'd been caught.

She needed no further explanation. The usual male Bajan technical defense when caught like that was to attack the family member who had caught him. The woman was pleased. Mamma's solution legitimized the woman's right to the money and spared her further mistreatment.

Looking out from the front windows of Alethaville, I could see the Smith's house slightly to the left on the opposite side. She was bedridden, and in the time that I knew her, she did not participate in the outdoor life of the gap. During the terrible hurricane of 1955, her son, the master mechanic who kept our car running, lifted her up and brought her to lie down in the back bedroom that my sisters used. It was further evidence of my mother's connection to those around her. She wouldn't let the dear lady be terrified lying there in a dark bedroom all by herself as the wind and rain battered her house.

A short, muscular woman lived with her boyfriend behind the Smith's house. They gave an occasional service-of-song or a straight house-bram to which children were not invited. The service-of-song was at the time a form of social-religious gathering at which food and alcohol were sold. The bram was a dance party staged in people's houses. An entrance fee was charged, and food and alcohol were sold. The bram always took place on a Saturday night: calypso music swinging, people laughing and talking bare "shittalk," a Bajan form of discourse that was conducted in fluent patois and centered on just about any conceivable subject as long as it did not personally concern any of the participants. The conversation was fueled by rum and the pork chop, a centerpiece of Bajan cooking. The expression "bare shittalk" refers to the discourse conducted in its most concentrated form.

Not everybody could participate in bare shittalk up in our gap. Participants had to have outgoing personalities and had to be willing to make argumentative assertions with unbridled confidence and, generally speaking, in a loud voice that was accompanied by hand gestures signifying premeditated arrogance.

"Don Bradman couldn't bat. Now Frank Worrell was a batsman."

"Man, wuh you talking 'bout? You evah see Bradman flick a ball off he nose at de las' minute and sen' de ball to de boundary? Widout even moving he body?"

"You talking shite, yuh know. Worrell had grace and fluency. He used tuh dance down de wicket tuh de ball and jus' flick it wid he wrist, an' wen yuh look, de ball was at de boundary. I nevuh see Bradman do dat. Bradman had tuh pull at de ball hard as ass. He used to swipe. Dah en nuh artist. He had to wuk hard, proof dat he en had nuh talent like Worrell."

Such arguments rarely relied on any objective element to make the case. A preference for one of these two world-class cricketers was best established with a loud voice, artful cricketing motions, and the capacity to hold forth extemporaneously, employing assertions unambivalently.

Similarly, when a speaker made clear at a shittalking session I witnessed that he could drive a stick-shift truck without using the clutch, he did not employ facts about the mechanical construction of the engine. He simply started making the noise of a truck engine with his mouth (*vroom, vroom, vroom*), revving it up by pressing on an imaginary accelerator with his right foot. Then he slowed the engine with his mouth and moved the gear stick with his left hand. His right hand was on the imaginary steering wheel, and his left foot stayed stationary and, triumphantly, did not go anywhere near the clutch. The man demonstrated his argument.

"Man, I tell yuh, I kin change gears without touching dat kiss-me-ass clutch. All yuh have to do is listen to de engine, an' at de right moment, den downshift without de clutch."

The speaker then threw down the gauntlet as he bit into his pork chop.

"And none o' wunnuh cyan do dat."

That final statement was the concluding touch to the theorem that had been so cleverly drawn. That was bare shittalk up in the gap.

The bram was a unique way for some people to make a bit of money. No family with children ever gave a bram. Mamma couldn't stage a bram. It would have been unseemly for a married woman with six children, and a reverend as a husband, to have all that alcohol consumed in her house. On the other hand, she had no qualms about helping with the cooking of the food for the neighbor's bram. My mother saw it as a gesture of friendship to help a neighbor make the preparations. These were people trying to make ends meet by working hard, because putting on a bram was not a task for lazy people. My father never discouraged her from participating in this collective village work.

That couple who staged the brams also provided some amusement to neighbors on other Saturday nights, when she would start bawling and screaming because she was being beaten by her man. No one ever intervened, probably because it was hard to take them seriously, since all of a sudden the screaming would stop and things would just go quiet. The village consensus was that the couple were then making love. No one really knew. However he was lashing her, or as we used to say, however he was sharing lashes, none of them ever made her swell up in visible places.

While the standards in those days admittedly overlooked some domestic violence that is now not tolerated, nobody could be sure what transpired in that house.

When one morning the male occupant at a different house got so angry at his wife that he threw a rockstone—a uniquely Bajan projectile that combined features of rocks and stones and that was probably found nowhere else on the planet except on that island of Barbados—at their front door and cracked it, then people intervened. The explosive sound of the door's giving way to the determination of a rockstone thrown in abandoned earnestness convinced everybody the man was serious. He was breaking the rules that would have normally assured the maintenance of his privacy in yesteryear Barbados. After all, he was there in broad daylight "brekking up he own house." And everybody knew that a missile pelted like that and catching an unsuspecting bystander would cause serious harm. So they intervened. You couldn't throw rockstones like that up in Station Hill. The intervention wasn't based on any newfangled principles about curtailing domestic violence. Anybody living in Station Hill could have explained it.

"It only blasted common sense. Wuh yuh gon do, leh he kill somebody?"

"He mus' be drunk. He cyan see dat lil childrun up in hey runnin' 'bout?"

Besides the bram, the unmarried couple also periodically gave a service-of-song, otherwise known as a sing-in, a remarkable cultural event that I always thought reflected a confluence of the powerful influence of the church in Barbadian society and the strong need of the people to create social events that gave them something to do that amused them and kept them distracted. The service-of-song brought people together. The rum flowed, pork chops and fried chicken were in abundance, and the people sang hymns and chanted psalms to their hearts' delight. Usually, there was a master of ceremonies who was in charge of the music end of things. He was the individual to start off a particular hymn by half-saying and half-singing, "Three, four," which was meant to put down the makings of a rhythm. And that designated leader would establish a line of the tune that everybody would then take up.

The process required several years of experience in some Protestant church or other to have a practical working knowledge of the most common hymns and the most popular chants for psalms. That rarely constituted a problem, because no one around us in those days was a Catholic. In fact, the only Catholics I knew then were a few white boys at school and one or two people who had come from the other islands like Grenada or Saint Lucia. Encouraged by the effective loosening quality of some dark Mount Gay or some "see-through" Alleyne Arthur rum, and reinforced by a stout or a bottle of beer, it was only a question of time before the haunting strains of the old-time hymns would be conjured up for immediate use. But of course, the other requirement of a successful service-of-song was that those present be able to sing a tenor or a bass line, for example. Hymns in unison didn't cut it. The mandate was for harmony, which in its fullness had to match the elegance of the pork chop preparation and the smoothness of the libation intermingled with some homemade pepper-sauce.

I actually got to attend in my boyhood days only one service-of-song, which was not held in Station Hill. Actually, this was an upper-class one that was conducted in a side street near Barry Springer's barbershop in the vicinity of the cathedral in town. I, and several of the treble members of the Cathedral Choir, had been invited by a bass chorister to show up and assure a strong soprano line at the affair. So we attended and found, to our surprise, that several well-known clergy and other distinguished members of the community were in attendance. We boys didn't drink, of course, but we ate and had cokes, or other "air-e-ated drinks, ef you please." This was something to see, because we performed. Not the usual hymns like "The Day Thou Gavest Lord Is Ended," or "On Jordan's Bank the Baptist Cried," or "Jerusalem the Golden with Milk and Honey Blessed," or "There Is a Green Hill Far Away." We went into the Psalms, beginning with the 23rd and then moving to the ones with complicated pointing, with the old-time upright lines and the dots that split words and sometimes phrases—indicating when the notes changed—and dictating rhythm.

There wasn't time that night for shittalk among the adults about who was running for the House of Assembly or how pretty some woman was. People had to concentrate on staying with the fellows, the sopranos from the choir. This was a high-class thing, and you had to know how to point. All of Gerald Hudson's training was on full display, and my father would have been proud of us, particularly since he always said that Hudson was the best choirmaster on the island at the time, with all the initials behind his name like ARCM and FRCO. We had to get really hot and show off, because a few people there started to trot out credentials and talk about how they sang in Saint Mary's Choir and Saint Leonard's Choir. Such self-promotion was patently offensive and ridiculous, because they were suggesting that their background and experience were up to ours. We had to take them on and show them what singing at a sing-in was all about and to make it clear to them that they were unlikely ever again to witness a performance like that. When we hit them with "The Lord Is My Shepherd," with the appropriate accent on "Lord," and then emphasized the first syllable of "shepherd," while letting the second syllable just hang there delicately—these false pretenders couldn't take the pressure. And no shouting from us. The tenors and the basses had to lighten up and follow our lead in the dynamics. This was Cathedral Choir work. You should have seen men that night regretting they were so far gone into the rum. As we all know, rum can make one's singing robust. But in that instance, the emphasis was on finesse and delicacy. This was time to show the uniqueness of the boy's voice, a world away from any other kind of soprano. Those men, in the midst of their darou, whether it was dark brown or see-through rum, were still collected enough to recognize when they had mistaken the dynamic interpretation of the lines. They appreciated that they had gotten their money's worth of the one-and-six (a shilling and sixpence) they had each paid as an entrance fee. My father was always proud that he too had been a boy chorister in the Cathedral Choir, and he clearly felt it special that his three eldest sons had passed through the same choir.

Located just opposite Alethaville was a house in which the Bico Steelband practiced. The house was under construction for a long time and still remained in an unfinished state that suited everybody. It had been placed on a lot that lacked clear configuration. If the house had ever been finished, it would have been forever behind other houses, with no definitive track leading to or from it except a path caused by the repetitive treading of human feet. In other words, no architect except a blind one would have put the house there. But somehow the Bico boys gathered in this half-built house with their instruments, which meant that all throughout the day, someone was practicing his part. If you consider that not one of those boys had any contact with music as a language of sorts, then it's clear that constant repetition was the only way to get to proficiency. The notes wafted through the air and entered Alethaville with a constancy that was surprisingly not irritating. I never ventured into that Bico house even out of curiosity, because I knew an unspoken rule dictated that I would not play steel-pan with the Bico group or with any other. Of course, this was long before the steel-pan entered the island's schools and even girls started playing. In my day, there was also mystery about who brought over the instrument from Trinidad and provided the hand patterns for the local boys to learn.

I knew my father well enough to understand the rules, even though he had not enunciated them lucidly. It was clear that I had to be in school, and in church school on Sundays. After school, I had homework and choir practice and other activities like the Boy Scouts. I could not have persuaded him that playing in a band of that sort promised something constructive and useful for my future. That was how he reasoned, and it was his duty to make the link for the son between present-day activities and what the future might hold. My father, like most Bajan men of his generation, was suspicious of unconventional paths to success. He liked outcomes that were linked to traditional schooling or on-the-job training programs. He understood that clergy were trained at Codrington College and that masons or jewelers participated in serious apprenticeship programs. But he had no grasp at all of where the Bico Boys' constant practicing would lead.

One other source of music in the village was the famous Colts Club. I have always assumed it was a common phenomenon in Barbados, this setting up of small clubs that served as venues for adult recreation during the weekend nights. Reverends like my father would not have gone there, of course, but lots of other village men went there, as well as village outsiders. Going there was not quite the same thing as leaving home to attend a dance in Queen's Park or at the Drill Hall. The Colts had a distinctly local flavor, which influenced the way patrons dressed and how much money was spent.

I never saw the inside of the Colts when it was in full swing; it was not a place for youngsters. My father would simply have thought me mad if I had set foot there. We had no need of a rule about the Colts. My father had had an incisive enough effect on my sense of propriety that I needed no regulation to inform me that I did not belong inside the Colts. That didn't prevent me from imagining that the dancers held each other in tight embraces, sweating hard while grinding to calypso rhythms, and making the most of the night before moving inconspicuously to the nearby cane-ground, because few people had cars or other mechanisms that assured the necessary privacy.

My father was a definite presence at home even when he was out. Mamma's occasional reminder that she would tell him about some misdemeanor or other was enough to reinforce his values when he was not there. So I could not have gone either to the Colts Club or to the Bico practice shed.

CHAPTER FOUR

Hauling Pots

They that go down to the sea in ships, that do business in great
waters; these see the works of the Lord, and his wonders in the deep.
Psalm 107:23-24

My father and mother decided one day that it would make
sense to send us children to pass the long school vacations in
Road View, which is the name of a strip of road that hugs the
Barbadian coastline in the northern parish of Saint Peter. The decision
resulted in my being exposed to a different side of life in Barbados, a culture that most boys living in Station Hill would never have seen. Just as
many of us make the mistake of thinking that everybody in the United
States lives like New Yorkers or everyone in France follows the trends of
Paris, I was surprised to find that Road View, Saint Peter, was so distinctly different in culture from Station Hill, Saint Michael. Even
though Barbados is small, with all its 166 square miles housing about a
quarter of a million people, life in the multiple pockets of the island is
a study in contrast. So while transportation experts would point out that
Station Hill was a mere handful of miles away from Road View, probably no more than twenty minutes away as the crow flies, the two villages
were strikingly dissimilar in the early 1950s.

Road View itself was little more than a small slice of the main highway that ran from Eagle Hall corner in Saint Michael all the way past Speightstown in Saint Peter. There was nothing grand about this central artery that connected the north and south of the island, so "highway" is an exaggeration. Indeed, no terminology comes to mind that does Road View justice in describing accurately its function first as a public way for the passage of all manner of locomotion. It permitted a single lane of traffic in both directions, and cars used it, as did bicycles, donkey carts, lorries carrying canes, and walkers facing the hot sun. It served, too, as the main bus route. But "highway" does not convey the essential idea that houses were placed on both sides of this byway at no more than a few feet from the road's edge, thereby converting the area into a small village. In other words, highway or not, the artery ran through the village of Road View. There was little depth on the seaside, and the houses on that side were usually squarely placed on the beach. But on the upper side, as Roadviewers called it, I had to look carefully to recognize that there was more than just the row of houses lined up on the side of the road.

Drivers who understood that Road View housed village life would slow down, inherently recognizing that people were expected to be lounging at the side of the road talking. Or a woman might be walking along with her child on the way to some event that was important in their lives and unaware of the right-of-way given to vehicular traffic. Bus drivers clearly knew that there was life along that road, and it was a common occurrence to see one stop his bus and suddenly cry out.

"Mrs. Jones, Mrs. Jones, Archie from up by Saint Stephen's Hill tell me to gih yuh dis package. He say he en get de res' yet. De res' comin nex' week."

"Bosie bo, t'ank yuh, hear. I did waitin' fuh dis. Now I kin gih my chilren someting tuh eat dis week. De Lord sho duz provide. Tell Archie t'anks."

The driver had done a kind deed and delivered the parcel for Mrs. Jones from Archie. Mrs. Jones had come out running to collect her parcel, appreciative that the gracious driver had agreed to do her a favor that was obviously not included in his list of job responsibilities. Another day, on his return trip going up to town, Mrs. Jones would flag him down and give him a parcel.

"Mr. Bynoe, de fish was plentiful yesterday. I was thinkin' 'bout you an' I know you an' yuh family could do wid sum uh da kingfish I put in dis parcel fuh yuh. Besides, wunnah cyan get sweet sweet fish like dis up in town. I even clean it fuh yuh so dat yuh missus don' have to break she back in de kitchen. De Lord be wid yuh."

This was Road View's form of reciprocity, parcel for parcel. The driver no doubt enjoyed the gift of fresh fish, a gift to recognize his kindness. This was village life, adhering to its own rules and adapting to the needs of the people.

A gas station was located on the right going north, just after the beach area now called Mullins. The station generally defined for us the beginning of Road View. An old cemetery on the right hand marked the end of the village, and one encountered the burial ground before entering Speightstown. The village therefore stretched about a mile. In the village was located one small Pentecostal church, which drew its congregation from an area wider than the village. Most of the houses were small, although unique larger ones stood out at certain points along the way. I know that some people may have difficulty envisaging Road View as a self-contained village area, especially since it was inherently a part of a main road on which traveled every day thousands of people going to and returning from Bridgetown, the main city located to the south. But those travels had little to do with the lives of Road View's citizens.

My parents may have decided to send us to Saint Peter in order to broaden our education or simply to free them for a short period of time from the work of caring for us. It might even have been intended to facilitate our connection to Mamma's side of the family, which turned out to be one of the outcomes of the decision, as we all got much closer to Esme. She was Mamma's cousin through some linkage to Mamma's mother and maternal grandfather, the famous Pa Hinds. Before I learned about Road View, Mamma's side of the family was less palpable, more difficult to hold onto than my father's relatives.

One of those unforeseen by-products was that Esme's husband always captivated me. Ozzie had no strict bloodline connection to us but was someone who exerted influence and impact through his gentleness, which stood in striking conflict with his muscular frame. He did not look at all like my father, although in many respects, I saw my father in him. Ozzie's was a physique well over six feet and further highlighted by his jet-black skin, which covered rippling muscles kept in shape by hard work at the neighboring sugar factory. He also had no noticeable midriff, no belly, no paunch to detract from his musculature. This image of an imposing, powerful man was further enhanced when I met his brothers, who were all just as tall, arresting athlete types. In fact, one of the brothers was actually a boxer, although I have no idea what his performance was like in the ring. Seeing the brothers together always reinforced my belief that their parents must have both been enormous physical specimens.

Some men, because of their imposing physiques, infuriate other men and provoke fights. In contrast, Ozzie's size and manner were veritable tranquilizers wherever he went. People felt protected in his shadow, and children like me were drawn to him in imitative wonderment. It must have been the quietness of his strength that made me reflexively think of my father. Both of them conveyed the message that I was protected in their charge, that there was nothing to worry about once they were around.

Ozzie's value in my mind increased once I got to know Esme better. His choice of such a unique woman reflected either remarkable insight or a special blessing. She was a dark-skinned, self-effacing woman of short stature, with a slightly protruding abdomen and an ever-present smile. She wore a straw hat most of the time, as much to protect her from the sun as to make it easy for her to push her hair under the hat and not worry about whether it was carefully combed. And she loved going without shoes, a practice that obviously toughened the soles of her feet and also allowed her toes to spread out, enjoying the unconfined space usually imposed by footwear. In her billowing three-quarter-length skirts, she walked with unconcerned ease, each foot gently placed laterally to the other, not like the young women working in town who placed one foot in front the other, carrying themselves "like dey seize up."

Once I saw her and Ozzie together, it was hard to stifle the thought about how physical opposites so often inexplicably attract each other. Esme walked in her husband's shadow, but not the way current-day feminists would mean it. She was proud of her husband and knew that he was a big man who cast a long shadow wherever he went, which did not dilute the authority she exercised in many arenas of their relationship.

She just basked in the unspoken protection of his being. This does not imply that she needed protection from anybody in Road View in the early 1950s. But to a child's mind, if she were to ever need protection, then it would be there. Everybody knew her husband. So to bother her and then have to deal with her man later on was just not imaginable.

In that era, it was natural for me to think that Esme's calmness had something to do with the qualities of her husband. She radiated peace and, from time to time, translated her irritation with someone through nothing more that a sharp sucking of the teeth, a country version of the "chupse." Then she'd turn her back, say to no one in particular, "Don't mind she," and walk off, her dark eyes flashing. That was the extent of her tantrum.

Ozzie and Esme behaved as though they were collective partners on a long expedition of some sort. Nevertheless, each partner had unique roles to fulfill, a defining difference from what some modernists advocate. My mother and Esme had responsibility for the running of the house and the care of the children. But it was important in the Barbados of that time for everyone to know that Ozzie was the man at his house, and that my father resided at Alethaville. And when in Road View village, I said I was staying with Ozzie, people instinctively warmed up to me. I immediately had standing. Up in town, I had long since appreciated what it meant to announce in certain contexts who my father was. This brings me back with sorrowful contemplation to what it must have been like for other children who did not have a father. I could not have that experience even when I was away in Road View, because my father's image was too strongly impressed on my child's mind. But Ozzie's presence was a catalytic replacement for my own father.

Ozzie did not lose his temper easily. I did see him on one occasion display his protective qualities. A feral cat had entered the house and was walking around on the crossbeams found in those small country wooden houses, where centipedes and scorpions sometimes were in hiding. Ozzie took a metal walking stick he kept in the house and pushed me out of the way, while explaining that feral cats sometimes attacked if they felt cornered. Then he raised the cane and with one blow struck the cat unconscious. It was a decidedly uncomplicated but definitive act. I was safe, the cat was no longer a threat, and Ozzie returned to his usual charming nonchalance.

Years later, when I went to visit him and Esme on one of my return visits to the island, I could not stand seeing him with the characteristic flexed arm and the rigidly dragged leg of the stroke victim. It was a terribly flawed version of my Ozzie, and I did not like it at all. Such simple kind men ought not to be so humiliated before they leave us.

My good sense tells me that he and Esme had arguments like every other couple in the world. But I never saw it. The other thing that seemed so evident was their unbridled respect for my father and Mamma. And they were clearly pleased to host us children for many weeks over a number of years. Since they had no offspring, it was evident that we brought life to their house during the long school vacation. None of us was so small that baby care was needed, and we all behaved responsibly. The major dangers to avoid were probably the traffic on the main road and the sea urchins on the reefs in the area.

Separation of the village into seaside and upperside made sense to me. Life on the seaside focused naturally on the expanse of the Caribbean Sea, where many people had a small boat called a moses lined up on the beach. The moses was used for "hauling pots," a peculiar local expression that described the use of pots for capturing fish. One did not raise the pot so as to retrieve the captured fish. One hauled the pot.

Esme and Ozzie lived at one time on the seaside. Later on, they moved up closer to the gas station, which is where they opened a shop on the inland side. The house on the beach side was so small that I am always puzzled to figure out retrospectively where all of us slept. There was no specific toilet facility, a clearly modern contraption that was essential to people in Saint Michael, "up in town" as Road View inhabitants used to say. But Road View had a beach and lots of trees. So the service rendered by the latrine was performed effectively by a trusted tide of water that cleaned up anything that was not buried properly. At night, a potty was available for people who were afraid to venture out in the dark.

A well in the yard provided us with water. I needed no warning about having to be careful not to skylark around the well, not to use it as a site for child's play. Small fish lived in the well, and I never found the words to explain how they would have arrived there. Perhaps some connection existed between the sea and underground fresh water in that area. When we moved to the house on the "above side," there was an outdoor latrine, without running water, of course. But that house was also closer to a standpipe located on the inland side of the main road.

Since we were on vacation, the day started whenever the noise from conversations being held outside were loud enough and when the sunlight streaming into the bedroom was strong enough to wake us up. Sometimes I got up much earlier when I decided to go hauling pots with the area's fishermen. Then I had to be dressed by five o'clock, when it was still dark outside. The men said it was important to keep the location of their pots secret, so much of the work was done under cover of haze and twilight. Even then I didn't believe that explanation, because they knew that coastline like the back of their hands, and I thought they could all find each other's pots with a minimum of effort. But the darkness did help with the ambience and the mystique surrounding the activity, and it certainly kept me enthralled, boy from up in town as I was.

I was clearly a town boy, and I recognized that the minute I set foot in a moses. I had to learn how to handle the oars. Rowing is very much an art form, especially for boys who lack the mature muscle power of grown-ups. I had to learn how to make the oars strike the water at an angle that would not provide so much water resistance that I would tire myself out in five minutes. On the other hand, obtaining no resistance at all meant that the oars were being kept practically at the surface, and the moses would stand still. Then I graduated to sculling—using a single oar on the back of the moses, an action that required skillful wrist work to move the small boat smoothly forward in a straight line.

The fishermen never trusted me to haul the pots up from the bottom of the ocean without falling overboard, which would not have been too amusing, since we were operating in very deep water that was a dark threatening blue because the sun could not penetrate the depth. But as I say that, I recall with some amazement that several of those fishermen in that day couldn't swim, a fact that always puzzled me and that made Ozzie seem even more heroic in my mind, since he possessed a powerful swim stroke that made him glide through the water.

In those days in Road View, it made sense for families to pool their money and support a fisherman who would run the moses and operate the pots that the group of families had bought. This investment assured many families a wonderful midday meal as well as some extra money from the sale of the fish. The biggest expense was in maintaining the moses. Sometimes a family member ran the boat, but several shared the expenses of keeping it seaworthy. There was also the cost of repairing the pots and furnishing the bait that attracted the fish to enter this metallic cage, from which there was apparently no exit.

From time to time I examined these pots, these metallic cages, from end to end, driven by my inability to understand the behavior of fish. I could not fathom how the fish, in pursuit of the bait that attracted them, could find the funnel entrance to the cage but couldn't turn around and just swim back in the opposite direction up the funnel to freedom in the open sea. I thought them hopelessly foolish, unforgivably so, since their behavior led inexorably to their deaths. And then, why could the ones caught inside the cage not send a message to their brothers and sisters outside, telling them to avoid these metal devices that were so utterly destructive to the fish families? This was boy reasoning, boy argumentation. But it seemed so obvious to me then.

Hauling pots was not like deep-sea fishing for flying fish or barracuda. Neither was it like standing on a reef close to shore and throwing a net to catch small fish. Manipulating that net was a skill to be acquired after lots of practice, and I never did it. Hauling pots was its own specialized activity, with its own culture and secrecy. It happened under cover of darkness, and the necessary skills got passed on magically. Fishermen did not discuss openly the characteristics of the best place to drop a pot. They did not argue in public about what constituted the most useful markers of where they had dropped their pots. I was curious about all this and would only learn a few of the secrets during each vacation period.

One of the principal objectives when people woke up in Road View was to determine what was going to make up the noon hot meal for that particular day. Since few people in Road View had a fridge, as they used to call it, most of the ingredients of that main meal had to be fresh. That's why Road View's obvious proximity to the sea led inevitably to the consideration of fish as a steady part of the diet.

Families in Station Hill also concentrated energetically on this central question of what they were going to eat. But they considered a wider array of options: corned beef and salmon from the tin; a slice of salt fish from the village shop; some Spam. Road View women had less money to spend at the shop. More consideration was given to what the village fishermen had to offer. And with the obvious absence of middlemen, such an option was cheaper and made more sense for the economy of that village.

The fish came in multiple forms and sizes, and the women cooked them in different ways. When money was tight, the women would fry jacks and sprats, the smallest fish available. The coalpot was still reigning in Road View, outside in the yard, giving off smoke and aromas of whatever was being prepared. Families took advantage of all the breadfruit, yams, potatoes, and other natural produce that those on the above side, away from the sea, might have been cultivating. That's when I saw in concentrated fashion the roasting of breadfruit and corn on the coalpot.

Few Road View citizens ate the lobsters we occasionally found in the pots. In fact, it was years before I realized that people ate lobster. I remember one day in Saint Kitts, I sat watching a local woman suck the meat out of every crack and crevice of a lobster. It reminded me of Road View families and their fish heads. The noise was similar, as was the obvious sign of pleasure on the eater's face. But the dish was clearly different. Lobster was an outcast in Road View. I have no idea why that was so, particularly when I notice the price of lobster these days and also note that I've eaten lobster as a common dish in Grenada, Haiti, and other islands. But never in Road View, where everybody ate much of whatever the sea provided.

Culture from up in town still penetrated Road View every day when a man pushing a Zephirin Bakery cart came along. We ran to it, looking for something that would meet the definitional test of dessert. Not dessert in a formal sense, since that was never a part of Road View meals, but something to sweeten a boy's mouth. The bakery man usually had turnovers, rock-cakes, jam-puffs, and other pastries whose names I have long forgotten.

I have made the mistake of trying, on return trips, to recapture the taste of a rock-cake or turnover. But I have had to concede that either my taste for such fare has been withered by other experiences in the years elapsed since then or the present-day turnover or rock-cake is just a pale imitation of what was produced in yesteryear. I will not accept the notion that my memory has distorted the taste and quality of a rock-cake or turnover from my youth, making those desserts better than they really were.

Road View's essential geographic characteristic was its location on the sea, a point that was obvious then to visitors like me. But the simplicity of that assertion was not a fact that I felt the citizens of Road View fully appreciated. Nobody in Road View was in a position to suggest that his or her beach was as white and pretty as anything to be found on the southern coast of France or the California coast of the United States. Road Viewers could not make those claims, not having seen any of those places. So I waited many years before I could make those claims on my own. While still growing up in Barbados, I had to figure out by myself that the water off Road View was among the best to be found in Barbados, especially since it lacked the riotous waves seen off the parishes on the east coast.

I took as my private and personal domain the beach off the road going south, in the new Mullins area. The sand was fine and a deep cream. It hurts now to pass by there and to see how the developers have taken over my beach, and the foreign tourists rent beach chairs and broad parasols to protect them from the sun, and they pay for drinks to be brought to them. It is no longer my beach, nor apparently the beach of any Road View villager. There is no longer anything serene or quiet about it, anything secret. I have lost my childhood space, and my birthright has been bought right out from under me. They tell me it is the obligatory price of progress, of having an island that sells or rents itself to foreign tourists.

The only problem about my beach was that on entering the sea, three or four steps could in some spots take a bather swiftly into deep water, which was particularly problematic for the unprepared. In that area, a few people, probably whites, had moored their small sailboats. I say the boats belonged to whites, because I knew no blacks with craft that were used for pleasure. I used the boats as a marker point to which my friends and I could swim and then turn around. Markers were always comforting when we were swimming in the open sea. They gave us a sense of control, of being confident about where we were and how that related to our swimming strength.

Esme did not go into the sea with us. Ozzie did it once or twice, as did a few other men I knew in the village. The beach was explicitly given over to the youngsters in the village, and we played cricket or football on it. The adults kept a certain lore about the sea in their vocabulary. They told us where the tide was strongest, which rocks had sea urchins and therefore should be avoided, what trees on the beach were poisonous, where we could find seashells with the most unusual colors. After showing how much they knew about the local area, the adults still hesitated to go in, to take a sea bath that the people up in town used to recommend so assiduously as healing balm for all sorts of ills.

As Road View adults predicted, after hours and hours of playing in the sea and not "washing off" properly, my skin began to get rough and scaly and dry and ashy-looking, a peculiar kind of off-white. It was fit punishment, because I was too tired after three or four hours of playing in the sea to walk to a standpipe and rinse my skin in fresh water. So the salt would stay on and do its job of transforming my skin into something that Road View mothers didn't quite like. Scaly skin didn't respond well to Vaseline, and it also made young boys look dirty and uncared for, as though they didn't have attentive mothers.

It all made little difference to me. I was more interested in the play. Youngsters can think up a spectrum of games to be played in the sea and on the beach that defy classification. And if the sea is calm, as Road View's water generally was, and the youngsters can swim, then the games are played with even more assurance and confidence, since there is much less treachery to be expected from a friendly sea. As the folklore had it, people in Road View didn't drown the way swimmers did in Saint John and Saint Philip, where waves were man-high and people talked about undertides and so on. At certain points in Saint Peter, you could stand on the road and see the bottom of the sea, a sign of the water's placid nature and faithful translucency.

In fact, Road View's water, that is to say the sea in Road View, became a reference point by which I measured all sea after that. I know that people all over the world talk about their sea and beaches, but I say confidently that none of it matches what Road View had to offer me as a little boy. Road View had pure transparent water that stimulated a search for adjectives to capture the multitude of blues and greens reflected off the surface. Sections of the sea had slight waves, and other areas had some bigger waves. But there was never a wave to evoke fright or terror. This wasn't Saint Philip or Saint John, where people had to be warning children all the time. Road View was for lovers of the sea, not warriors. No surfing was done there. No need for muscles and showing off that you could conquer the sea. This was for the placid contemplation of a rock being thrown by a little boy like me, the rock skipping delicately across the surface, touching three or four times before finally parting the water and slowly sinking to the bottom, engulfed by the water that then returned to its original shape. And miraculously in Road View, no woman who dared to enter the water there ever looked ugly doing so. Road View's sea transformed every woman into a majestic creature just through the act of her stepping into the water.

Sometimes, accompanied by my older brothers, I walked along the beach from Road View all the way to visit school friends whose parents had a bayhouse in Saint James. It was easy to do that when the tide was low. I admired the fancy houses we walked by. I picked up stones of different shapes and colors that had been simultaneously polished by the sea and eaten into by marine life I did not understand. Once finished admiring them, I would throw them back into the water. It was a time of glorious freedom and pleasure. No obligatory hour to get back home. No adults to worry about something bad happening. When we got to our friends in Saint James, we found more youngsters to play with. And cokes and crackers and cheese to keep our energy up, and even a Ju-C, the local drink that came in deep red or yellow. Some administrator recently decreed that Ju-Cs should no longer be manufactured, and I wondered whether he or she understood the profound cultural and historical impact of the decision. Getting rid of Ju-C drinks was an act of cultural malice. Ju-Cs were a part of my childhood, uniquely fitted to the tropics, by sweetness, distinctive colors, and volume. At school, one ordered a Ju-C with precision from the hawkers in the schoolyard. No one asked for a Ju-C the way one ordered a coke. Qualifiers had to be there, generally through the color. Some boys liked a red Ju-C; others wanted a yellow one. Each color had its partisans.

I have heard in recent years that construction projects along the northwest coastline of Barbados have ended up with big boulders being put on the beach that block the path of anyone strolling there. As a result, beach promenades over long distances have now been rendered difficult. In the 1950s, nobody discussed the vision of protecting these pleasures and privileges for the simple folk like those in Road View.

None of us ever imagined it would be necessary to protect a villager's access to the sand and the simple unadulterated joy of strolling on the beach and talking back to one's own inner voices. It may have been necessary on the beaches up in town, where expansionists at the private yacht clubs wanted to safeguard the beach for their white members. But not in Road View.

When night fell in Road View, the village took on a look that was copied in many areas of Barbados in that era. Some families had electricity and others didn't. In the first house, Ozzie and Esme used kerosene lamps. Then later on, they were connected to the light switch. Kerosene lamps threw light over a limited space. If the chimney needed cleaning, or the wick was throwing off a lot of smoke, the area covered by the light was in turn diminished. From the outside, the houses illuminated by lamps always took on a funereal atmosphere, which added to children's fear of the dark and fed their beliefs that spirits moved around at night. That is no doubt why in lamp-lit villages, people congregated on the steps in front of their houses to chat. Or men got together under public lights to play games like dominoes. Congregate human contact diluted the anxiety provoked by having to move around darkened houses. Furthermore, families rarely lit more than two lamps per house. This meant that only mandatory activities got the light. The rest was handled in the dark.

An important distinction between the two houses that Ozzie and Esme lived in rested on the lack of a radio in the first and the presence of Rediffusion in the second. With no radio, Ozzie often brought out his guitar when he returned from work, after the sun went down and he had taken a sponge bath and had eaten what Esme had prepared for him. He had a strong, distinctive strum, and for a man whom I had never seen dance, his mastery of calypso rhythm was impeccable. He had a way of singing that suggested he was half-drunk, like the way the old-time calypsonians in Trinidad used to sing. I knew he wasn't drunk, because Ozzie could hold his liquor, and in any case, he would never reach that state during the week when he had to work the next day. It was just that he sang that way, gravel-voiced, slightly obfuscating the note, half-swallowing the lyrics while maintaining the precise beat that was necessary for his dancing audience to enjoy themselves. This was the time when "Adam in the Garden Hiding" and pieces like "Kitch, Come

Go to Bed" were in full sway, long before Bajan calypsonians had taken their turn to be creative and write their own songs.

I was resolutely upset when they had Rediffusion installed, and Ozzie put down his guitar and didn't take it up again. He told me once that the music coming out of that box was enough, and he couldn't compete with it. It is true the box brought the news and a short religious service, during the weekday morning and on Sundays, which Road View appreciated. After all, we didn't have to make up our own daily prayers. We could lie in bed and have the minister say a prayer, and we could say Amen at the end and have fully participated in giving God thanks. Rediffusion also brought cricket scores right into the house, so we wouldn't have to walk down the road, stop by a shop, and ask for the latest numbers, who was batting and who was bowling, and how many runs needed to be made for any particular side to win. Rediffusion had some usefulness. But it shut down Ozzie and his guitar, and I concluded that the price for such technological progress was inordinately high. I never thought something like a radio could turn the life of a small village upside down. That is until they got the telephone, and people started calling up to make an appointment before they dropped by to see how you were doing, which gave the hosts a chance to invent an excuse to put off the visit. And so the spontaneous village house visit began to peter out, not right away, but slowly and progressively. Slowly enough that one could never say it was completely eliminated, and insidiously enough that only the very observant could even clearly notice what was happening.

During my time in Road View, there was still spontaneity about the act of connecting socially to others in the village. One afternoon, everybody went on the upper side, the side not on the sea, behind some houses that were located along a track. In Barbadian parlance, a track is accessible to people on foot, or maybe to cyclists who had skill and experience with uneven surfaces. But a track will not accommodate a car. We stopped in an area that was open, as though it was designed by nature to be used by groups of people. And people did begin to assemble. The get-together was in the open, not in anybody's house or in anybody's yard. A few buckets made their appearance, and ice was placed in them. Then everything that was liquid and could possibly be drunk was poured in: falernum—that sweet Bajan liqueur, the obligatory rum, stout, beer, soft drinks, some coconut water, everything. The ever-present lime was there too, because it was just naturally everywhere. And since the country Bajan must sweeten things, all things, someone added molasses or cane syrup that came from the neighboring sugar factory. It was mixed up and stirred and shaken up and stirred again. It was sweet, yet tangy and cold and just good, something a young boy like me had never tasted before, certainly not up in town in Station Hill.

There was no warning like what you get from the burning of plain rum or whisky going down inside you, telling you that it is a man's drink and boys ought to know their place. This was sweetness itself, served by women who always looked out for their children. It was a hot afternoon, so I had to drink something to quench my thirst, which would never be satisfied by anything sweet. I had a second glass. It was even better than the first, this time probably fueled more readily by the laughing and the talking and the wonderfully protective presence of adults I knew and trusted. I did not know how long it had been since I had taken the first glass. Suddenly, I realized I was unsteady on my feet, and my words were no longer properly formed and enunciated. At that point, I was likely drunk. But the next phase came quickly, with the swirling of the entire environment and a sort of half-nausea that didn't let me vomit easily and clear it all up. I was more sick than drunk, more sick than half-drunk then, and Esme quickly recognized it and started to comfort me and let me know she was there and there was nothing to worry about. Her voice did not calm me as much as she had hoped, since it was eerily distant and half-obliterated by Ozzie's guitar strumming. But I made it to the house all right, putting one foot hesitantly in front of the other. Weeks later, with much laughing, she let my father know how I'd been under the weather and why. He took it in stride, as by then it was water under the bridge, and I looked no worse for the experience. It was a fine early lesson for me about the subtle danger of alcohol.

A number of people in Road View offered me their friendship. In the evening, two sisters who were clearly much older than I sometimes took me to the pictures, that wonderful old-time name for the movies. The movie house in Speightstown, a short drive from Road View, was a tiny hall that looked like a former schoolroom, and certainly not like anything that currently passes for a cinema. There was a distinction between the pit and the rest of the house, as was the case in the grander

houses up in town. But that was a distinction without much of a difference. We didn't even sit on chairs, but on hard church benches that were
unpolished. We all sat close together, which fueled the totally imaginary
idea that I was on a date with a sophisticated woman. The picture on
the screen was grainy and full of lines. At least everybody was gentle and
not half as noisy as moviegoers were up in town. This was the country,
and I was pleased to be out.

Road View sensitized me to the place of rum in social intercourse.
People drank rum too in Station Hill, but I never noticed it as much,
and it did not seem to be the necessary catalyst of every social interaction. However, in Road View, rum had a special place that was defined
by cultural injunction and created by Road View's citizens: Wherever
there were people gathered together, rum should be served. And so it
was. I emphasize rum since I did not ever see another form of alcohol
used with the consistent frequency of rum. It was also clear that a significant accomplishment of manhood was knowing how to hold one's
liquor, because there were rules to be followed and fine lines to be
walked when an adult had in his darou. It was pointless to alert everyone to the fact that one had been drinking. One couldn't fire a couple
of drinks and then start cursing in front of Esme or me, a child, and
then apologize later on. Such unmannerliness was prohibited, as were
fights provoked by alcohol. In the midst of all the drinking, a man could
not touch another woman who was not his declared lover. Rum was
expected to loosen one's tongue and make one more poetic in argumentation, not render one more irritable and cross and a public nuisance.
One day a man showed me the place of rum in his life when he took
some and poured it on his head, claiming that it protected him from all
manner of ills and assuring me that rum had the medicinal property of
embalming the living.

Years later, when I was interested in the problem of alcoholism, I
struggled with the definition of that malady that wreaks such havoc on
populations worldwide. There must have been some individuals in Road
View whose social or work functioning was impaired by the steady consumption of rum. But that was hard to see then, because those who were
working did so assiduously. No work, no pay was a simple rule in those
days, and people had to work to eat. And as a child, of course, I certainly had no idea whether, for example, alcohol interfered with people's

marital relationships. I can imagine, however, that cirrhosis of the liver did occur, affecting the individual only much later in his life, and was likely presented to friends and family as some other more benign disease. No one used the words "alcoholic" or "alcoholism" at that time because such words may have been applicable to so many people that they would therefore have lost meaning because of their lack of precision. Alternatively, most people in Road View would likely have argued that such stigmatizing labels were meant to describe the man rolling in the gutter, "blind drunk" as they would say, unable to find his bearings to reach home. Such men were not citizens of Road View village.

I connected rum to men and not to women. Such fine distinctions were also part of Road View's cultural rules. Rum was a catalyst of male discourse. This is not to say that women did not drink. They did not consume rum constantly and persistently the way men did. It did not take me long to recognize that the word "woman" generally meant mother, even if it did not mean wife. Women took care of children and prepared meals and maintained a loyalty to their church and to the task of raising their children in a Christian household. Women had to keep their wits about them in the morning. If the fishermen didn't bring in the kind of fish anticipated that day, then every woman had to "stir she hand" and figure out what she was going to cook in the place of the missing fish. This was short-term strategic planning, and a drinking woman wouldn't be able to handle such sharp thinking. Another crucial point was that rum made the men talk loud and boast. Mothers didn't do that in Road View, unless they were pointedly angry with someone and for some reason.

Women cared about how their peers perceived them, and behavior instigated by Mount Gay or Alleyne Arthur rum was all right for men, but not for women.

I remained on the lookout for rum after my stay in Road View, always wondering about why it had to be present for people to enjoy liming together, just "hanging out," talking and laughing. I went to post-funeral receptions and realized how important rum was to the success of the event. At some funerals, more rum was consumed than at some of the wedding receptions I witnessed. At the funerals, it was as though rum was employed as a libation to the gods, and the men all dressed up in black suits drank nervously and with a peculiar, driving insistence. This was not the jocular consumption of rum so common to the wedding reception.

On a return visit to Road View many years later, I stopped at the beach bar at Mullins to have a drink and seek some information about a family I wanted to locate. I met a local citizen and struck up a conversation about Road View and the people I was looking for. The local chap did indeed know the family, many of whom had died. But one member of the clan still remained, and I was directed to the individual's house down the way off the main road on the above side, or to a rum shop, which was the other likely place to find the individual. The man I was seeking was not at the rum shop, a fact that was determined by simply shouting out the individual's name.

"I lookin' for Joe. He dere in de shop?"

The answer came ringing back to me from inside the shop. "No, he en here. Check he out home."

I did so, having to park my car and use a track that took me past a few houses to where my man was located. My guide, the one I had met at Mullins, didn't abandon me. He stayed to be helpful and to get a drink from a bottle he knew would be there at the house I was looking for, since the man I was seeking was well known to have a bottle available for guests. I did find Joe at home, seated on the floor of his little living room, which was clearly the safest place for him. He was in no condition to stand up and negotiate any space on his own. This was the closest I got to problematic drinking in Road View, and I felt sorry for him. But it made me wonder if I had missed all this as a boy because vigilant family members had kept it hidden from outside eyes.

I was always struck by this difference between the Road View use of rum and its place in Alethaville. Both my father and Daisy used rum in this peculiar fashion of opening up their appetite. They claimed it settled their stomachs, made them eat comfortably and enjoy the taste of the food more. Apart from that midday ritual, my father took a drink when his friends visited. But he rarely took more than one, and he certainly never shared it with any of us children. Consequently, I was surprised when he said nothing to me after hearing about my experience in Road View, and I concluded that he did not wish to offend Esme or Ozzie.

Anyone who spent more than a month or so eventually came into contact with the village's special characters, individuals who were unforgettable even after one encounter with them. My attraction to them may have been fueled partly by my status as a transient. Station Hill did not have personalities of this genre; and if they existed, they could not have been part of my life in the same way the Road View individuals were. The powerful presence of my father in Station Hill would have made things different.

Tourist was a solidly built man, handsome in his own way, with a ring of gold around one tooth in the front of his mouth that, coupled with his singsong way of talking, highlighted the fact that he was Trinidadian. He sometimes slept in the house, which probably meant he was a distant relative of Esme or Ozzie. He was a mason, and I went with him one Saturday to watch him work on a construction project in Saint James, where he kept up an ongoing, saucy exchange with some of the women working at the site.

"You know you look sweet," Tourist would say in his calypso-accented manner.

"I know I look sweet," the object of his attention replied cavalierly. "And why that interest you?"

"Your sweetness bothering me. Dah is all."

"But why it bothering you? I en interfering with you," the woman noted, as she nonchalantly but provocatively passed her right hand over her pubic region.

"I just wondering if I could get some of the sweetness for my tea," Tourist added plaintively. This ability to move between metaphors was a necessary characteristic of men who wished to engage in sweet talk.

"I en want nuh man who en staying. You want free sugar for your tea. But it dis cost money to mek sugar up in any plantation 'bout here." The women, too, could switch metaphors easily.

"But wuh you got against me? Why yuh so stingy?"

"Dah fuh lick ya. I en stingy. But you want freeness. I en a idiot, yuh know. I cyan let you tek advantage of me. Some of you men tink every eyeful have to be a bellyful."

Tourist knew the woman liked him. But she wanted at least some modicum of a commitment, something he couldn't make before he got the sugar. His smooth tongue kept him at the center of much of their conversation. In addition, his brown skin and wavy hair obviously tickled women's fancy. I did not know why he was called Tourist, but I drew my own conclusion that it had something to do with his wonderful walk and the way he could work while appearing totally relaxed. In fact, he did everything in this special way of his that was clearly oriented to catch the eye of the women around him. He was no Bajan, and that stood out in this little village. I saw him with no particular woman, although I believed that he visited women at night on his bicycle when I wasn't using it. It wouldn't have made sense to bring any woman to Esme's little house anyway, not with all those inquisitive eyes and the circumscribed space.

Another favorite of mine was the Professor, or Mock Uncle, who would visit Road View proper from time to time. He liked to joke that he was my uncle because of some associative connection between our last names. Knowing that he was not a relative, we called a truce and settled for the mock designation. He lived off the main road as you went north toward Speightstown, with a jet-black woman who had two beautiful grown daughters from a previous alliance.

Mock Uncle was tall and thin and graceful. At another time, he would have been called well educated, which all Road View agreed was the case before something happened that reduced his status in the outside world, beyond Road View, something I knew nothing about. For me, he still turned a phrase with elegance and with an accompanying manner that was meant to show that he had style and he knew how things were done. He had social grace, and he was one of those who used rum to increase the fluency of his language. Children flocked to him, the same way they followed Tourist. Both of them took the time to talk to us, laughing and stroking our heads, turning us into people who deserved to be seen and heard. I wondered what the Professor was like as a young man and how he had gotten his education. How advanced it was I did not know and could not have figured out. In the world of Road View and in my eyes, he made it seem as though he had been once at Oxford University.

"Good morning, Mistress Downes," the Professor would announce, using Esme's family name by marriage, a name few people uttered. "And how does this lovely, sunny morning find you?"

The British-accented articulation would discombobulate Esme for a few seconds before she found her acid-tinged tongue, one she reserved especially for the arrogant airs of the Professor.

"Professor, why you bothering me so early dis morning? I en got nuh time for you. You come 'bout here wid yuh long, lawling hands. But I got tuh stir some cou-cou for dese children."

"Forgive me, Mistress Downes. I shall not interfere with a woman pursuing her matronly duties with such determination. A good morning to you, Madam."

Another time, I came up on the Professor chatting with five or six men, close by to somebody's house, which accounted for the glass of dark rum in everybody's hand.

"Gentlemen," he intoned seriously, "you are offering an hypothesis, upon which we are clearly not agreed. Furthermore, there is clearly little logic to your claims."

"Professor, as usual, you talking down to we. But you en mek nuh blasted point yet. British politicians and the Colonial Office don' give two shites 'bout black people in Barbados. An' you know dat is a fact."

"My good man, there is no need to resort to obscene language to make your point. There is virginal youth in our midst."

"You tink dis boy never hear a curse word? You trying to change the subject. De British colonize yuh ass, and you talking like dem. But deh don' want yuh."

With that sad indictment, the group turned to a discussion about whether the local fishermen had made a good haul that morning.

There was no one I knew in Road View of an age that caused me to ask whether he or she was attending secondary school and intended to pursue a profession of some type. So I cannot say what the villagers' dreams were for their young people in the world of work. Esme and Ozzie had no children. And we never discussed what they quietly harbored inside as hopes for any young people in the village. Neither could I be certain of the villagers' connection to any specific church. But I know they used prayer to enhance their connection to God, and He was important to them. What was clear was their expectation that people in their world be fair and respectful to each other. Every house was unlocked throughout the day, and people came and went with nothing more than a word to the neighbor to keep an eye out as they went on some quick errand. The request to keep an eye out was meant to refer to the clothes hanging on the line outside, which the neighbor should remove if the rain started to fall. It was not meant that the neighbor should protect the house from thieves. Who would steal in Road View? Such a thought was preposterous then. And the word "gang," while certainly in the dictionary of that era, had no conceivable applicability to Road View.

Life, in a Road View sense, was simple. I never had the chance as a child to ask Ozzie or Esme what would happen to me if I wished to stay in Road View permanently. It is possible, of course, that my own parents had long since posed and answered such questions in their own minds. They were always amused when they came to pick us up at the end of our stay and someone would suggest they leave one of us behind. Road View was for a vacation, and their long-term vision encompassed more and saw beyond that country village on the sea, beautiful though it was.

Still, I have been forever taken by the notion of Road View's simplicity. The one or two white families who lived there were clearly a part of village life. Not mixed up in it in a way that suggested they were on the side of miscegenation, for example. But mixed up in it to the extent that Ozzie occasionally knocked on their door to ask a favor, which was granted without hesitation. And they fired a rum on each other's head, as they said, whenever they ran into each other in the right context, and as custom dictated.

I know no way of re-creating breadfruit being roasted on the beach. I know no one now who fries jacks and sprats and offers them up as a meal, accompanied perhaps by breadfruit cou-cou turned expertly, without even a microscopic lump left to offend. And the sense of security that permeated every nook and cranny has long gone, mocked and chronicled by the ever spiraling business of placing wrought-iron bars at every window and door. This reminds me that I never saw a policeman in Road View. People could tell you the location of a doctor, a teacher, the pastor, and of course the mortician. But the police station up the hill as you left Speightstown was there to house a few officers who investigated the occasional accident. They remained invisible to the villagers in Road View. But that was once upon a time. Road View was in a sense my first excursion away from my parents, when I did things silently and wondered what they would have said had they known that I had done them. It was an opportunity to experiment with my self-confidence and to see whether it was well grounded.

CHAPTER FIVE

The Odd-Pedal

Looking out from Alethaville, obliquely to the right, were two important houses. The one farther away housed Miss Garner and the young girl, Philoh, an unusual name pronounced with the accent on the last syllable and a short middle vowel in the first. Miss Garner was likely in her sixties at the time, although she was to my youthful eyes always an old woman. Not old and decrepit, but still old, with strong but weathered hands and wavy, light brown hair. Her skin matched the gold in her tresses, and the shimmering reflection of her plaits was always heightened whenever she stepped out into the Bajan sunshine. She also had a sharp little nose that suggested inter-marriage among her antecedents. Her build was slight, making her almost into a wisp of a woman. However, she moved about vigorous-ly, with dignity in her step, and she carried herself with an air of insou-ciance, always dressed in a billowing long skirt. Nothing ever seemed to bother her, which was unusual to me since she was not generally known to be a woman who was always in church. In those days, church membership was a prerequisite for a calm, relaxed demeanor.

Miss Garner ironed clothes for lots of people in the neighborhood and was the only woman in the gap who routinely pressed clothes using irons heated on coals. Her expertise was invaluable, because she knew how to starch shirts with the right amount of stiffness, to make you look like "you come from a good family." And her coalpot-heated irons never left a black mark or a smudge on any white shirt anywhere in that gap. Miss Garner knew her stuff and kept the secrets of her trade to herself, just like she never talked to anybody about where she had come from or whether she was ever married. She was one of those women everybody called Miss Garner, not Mistress Garner, although the title "Miss" was often an abbreviation for "Mistress" when dealing with the older age group. Miss Garner was the most adept user in the gap of the coalpot, since hers was always working and was a fundamental part of her employment activity. Its nonstop use also meant she could throw a sweet potato, still in its skin, on the coals to roast slowly and transform itself into a delicacy for us children.

Daisy Best, known always and only as Daisy and not to be confused with the owner of Alethaville, lived in the closer of the two houses and was next to Miss Garner. Daisy was a different character altogether. Dark-skinned and short but plump, she had long thick hair that she always kept tied up in a bundle under a hat or a head-tie. She wore those broad-heel shoes that laced up and which made her look like some English lady going about her duties in the main house at the manor. She and my father and Mamma must have worked out a special arrangement to have her work for them without receiving a clearly defined salary. But Daisy was there first thing in the morning to make tea and last thing at night to make tea again. This was just before she would go and perform her evening ablutions, pour that white powder all over her neck that would be so obvious on her dark skin, and then go off to the evening service at the Cathedral or at All Souls. Which church she went to depended on the lateness of the hour, the available transportation, and who was preaching. She was the first person to teach me about the fidelity of women to their preachers. Her face could instantaneously darken at the mention of one preacher's name and miraculously lighten at hearing another's. It was important to her, this business of supporting men of the cloth. Since this was long before women were allowed in the pulpit of the Anglican Church, it cannot be fairly said that Daisy's loyalty was influenced by the gender of the priest.

Daisy had taken her elementary school education very seriously. She spoke carefully and read voraciously, and she had a thorough knowledge of all the kings of England and their respective wives. In fact, she had a visceral connection to all things royal and British. She defended Princess Margaret when Margaret fell in love with the famous group captain, who had lost a toe or part of it in some military maneuver or other, which prompted Daisy to say in a huff that she didn't know what a toe had to do with being a man. She said this in a tone that left only the truly ignorant or the uninitiated to miss her intended meaning, and she spoke of this princess as she would have spoken about an unfortunate neighbor living in the gap. That was another reason she kept her hair long, because it reminded her of the days when she was young, and real men fought to get tangled up in her thick braids. She also told me, with the assurance of a teacher conveying knowledge that she knew I would never learn from my parents, of a philosophical point she held dear.

"Boy, no wife seriously committed to her marriage ever wears pajamas to bed. A Christian woman wears a nightgown."

She left her pronouncement at that, adding nothing else to spice up the pot. This was a shortcut to the bare simple fact, one on which I would meditate laughingly later on, and always with the image of Daisy in my mind.

Daisy helped raise the last child in our family, and she had a close link to an older brother, although for all of us, she was clearly another one of those surrogate mothers in the village life of Barbados. She never spanked any of us children, which didn't mean we didn't understand that we could never treat her disrespectfully and expect to get away with it. Daisy was one of us; she and we knew it, and she went on all the church bus excursions like one of our family.

My father and she worked out quite a particular understanding. She called him Mr. Griffith or Reverend Griffith, and they both regularly staged these mini-arguments, in the course of which he would accuse her of having swiped some of the rum from a Mount Gay bottle he kept in the bottom of the press in the dining room. Now at that time, he and she were the only ones in the house who drank the rum. So he could have bought a bottle for her, labeled it with her name, and left it for her to keep in the kitchen, which was her space. Instead of implementing such administrative simplicity, he opted for complexity. He kept only a single bottle in the house, and each empty bottle was in due time replaced. My father routinely claimed that his rum progressively diminished at a rate that was considerably faster than his drinking could have produced, and he eyed Daisy suspiciously. She, on the other hand, with a straight face and a devout Anglican one at that, would insist that he was in fact mistaken, a gracious way of saying that he was the only one in the house holding to this belief that someone other than himself was helping consume the Mount Gay.

On some days when he returned home for lunch, she would mockingly add insult to injury by drawing nigh to his chair, located just in front of the press, at the head of the dining-room table. She approached like the Anglican communion supplicant she was, head bent with humility and trusting in divine grace.

"Reverend Griffith, I would like to have some rum, please. I need to open up my appetite," she used to say.

She wanted some of his rum, from that special single bottle, that Mount Gay bottle, the one with the map of Barbados on its face. Then my father would consider the question, turning it over in his mind with an air of sustained gravity. He sometimes looked as though in dispensing the rum, he was participating in a criminal conspiracy with Daisy. At other times, he seemed to feel that he was involved in the unpardonably wretched act of corrupting her soul, which was unforgivable treachery coming from a man of the cloth.

While her face stayed unsmiling, Daisy's eyes made it clear that she saw nothing wretched about her having a drink with her meal. She didn't have to go far into the well-honed argumentation of Bajan Christians to remind me that Jesus attended marriages where wine was flowing. So she would turn to me and then to Mamma and back again, because Daisy knew she had my father boxed in.

"All right, Daisy, take some of the rum."

He had to give her the rum and show himself a man, a kind and gracious one at that. Sometimes he poured it. Other times, it was she who did it. But on each occasion, she gave him the coup de grâce with the look that stated, "So why would I have to steal it?" Both of them played the game for years, and watching them constituted important lessons on how to joke with a deadly serious face and how to joust intellectually with an opponent while using a minimum of words. They matched wits with each other while creating minimal fuss.

However, Daisy wasn't joking when she asked my father to help her deal with the man she lived with, who was feeling his oats and occasionally mistreating her physically. My father had standing in the community, and he demonstrated that time and again in the quietest way possible. Tests of his mettle, when he was not angry, were occasions to assert his will almost without seeming to do so. With him the outcome was as important as the technique employed to reach the conclusion. So he walked quietly up to Daisy's house and went around to the yard in the back. He had a conversation with Daisy's companion that was unheard by anyone. My father did not lift his voice, and the man did not react with any vigor at all. Their conversation had no witnesses, and my father knew that in those instances, he got what he wanted most effectively when the opponent was not embarrassed or belittled. His voice, therefore, never carried out of the yard. No threats or promises were recorded from either side. But the man moved to another house, and he did it quickly and without comment. I have no doubt he knew that a telephone call from my father would have had him quickly facing a few police constables from District A police station nearby. So the man kept his dignity and avoided the challenge. Besides, everybody in the village knew he'd come up from another island, which in those days was a mark against a man. Not a big black mark, but one nevertheless that had people judging him capable of undefined mischief. This village prejudice was never voiced. And it did not mean that these occasional outsiders were unwelcome or not nice. It just meant that these others were a bit more likely than the homegrown Bajan to stray from the straight and narrow.

Daisy was a practical, sensible Christian. She attended church faithfully on Sundays and every Wednesday night. She was resolute in keeping these appointments with her God, and she did not allow minor impediments to keep her from these commitments. She also drank her rum and lived with her partner and saw these activities as no contradiction of her profound religious faith. She had a way of making the church's precepts conform to fundamental village values. When over a period of time the church remained stubborn and she witnessed some sermon in which her Anglican priest affirmed the church's stand that was the object of Daisy's scorn, she snorted and turned her back on the precept with which she was at odds. She had no time to waste on silliness. She dispensed, through a shake of her head, with the Pentecostals' idea that a Christian woman shouldn't have a drink. And she didn't trust the Catholic dogma that had their priests doing without women. She had no faith in a man who renounced sexuality. Daisy knew its inherent value in nurturing the human spirit as well as the body.

"No man should be in a cold bed at night. God gave us to each other."

That was her view, and she then lapsed into silence. She had no more to say to the Roman pope, whose ideas would have destroyed Daisy's notion of what was necessary to make the daily life around Alethaville and in the gap quietly joyful.

The open space in front of Alethaville next to Mrs. Smith's house was the flattest and most even area in the gap. This meant that it was a prime surface for groups wishing to hold an open-air church service, which was a common Bajan ritual. These village meetings were not as large as those held in the central bus stand in Bridgetown or in the fish market in Saint Peter, which were areas that had substantial pedestrian traffic. Our gap was in a local residential section, so the class of open-air meeting held there was intended to be smaller and more directly personal and intimate. Five or six men and women would show up with a lantern or two and maybe a small table on which they would rest a Bible or a prayer book. There was an unstated agreement with those who lived in the houses nearby that radios would be turned off, and activities in the houses would grind practically to a halt so as to minimize the possibility of disrupting the service. Mamma would give us strict orders to be quiet; then she would turn off most of the lights in the house and park herself at the front window in an obvious front-row seat. She would also provide the occasional glass of water to the preacher who needed it. I was always persuaded that the organizers of these services chose this specific venue because it provided the necessary flat open space, but also because they knew that the Reverend lived in Alethaville. Consequently, their open-air ministry would be welcome.

The service followed a traditional format of prayer and testimony, accompanied by hymn singing and ending with a long sermon that usually exhorted listeners and bystanders to accept Christ as their savior. It was hard to tell how many souls were saved at those services, but the activity reflected impressive orderliness and cohesiveness about the village. For one thing, the singing always felt more directly honest to me. The prayers and testimony also required a higher level of commitment than what one encounters inside the usual church. Furthermore, the preacher had to try harder at his art because he had to hold the attention of people who were passing by on their way to do other things. If the preaching and singing were of inferior quality, the audience just moved on quietly.

I liked Reverend Smith, who held court in the bus stand on Sunday nights. I always admired his gall in making a pitch to people who had just come out of the night service conducted at their own churches. He was basically inviting them to compare his style to what they had just left, and I thought such courage was outlandish and provocative. Here he was telling the passers-by that what they had just come from wasn't quite the real thing, and they were lucky to confront another opportunity to get right with God. And he was offering it to them on a silver platter. In recent years, the Spiritual Baptists and their leader, Archbishop Granville Williams, have been conducting service on Saturday nights in town. He has had impact on the cultural and religious framework of the island in a fundamental way. It is hard to escape the obvious message that, for at least a segment of the population, it is more pragmatically functional to attend church by the side of the road, to borrow an expression from the calypsonian Sir Don, than to be out doing other things that wouldn't store up for them treasures in heaven.

Returning to Station Hill, I'm reminded that it is not accidental that so much of the children's lives in the gap were lived on the outside, in the open air, where it was warm and tropical and there was space for running and jumping and making the noise that so agreeably accompanied the interaction of healthy children. It was a naturally ordained solution to the problem of large families and small internal living spaces. For much of the time, six of us children lived with Mamma and my father in a house with three bedrooms. Other families had the same number of children, plus children's spouses and an occasional grandchild. The outdoors was a compulsory area of activity; otherwise the seriously cramped indoor space would have driven people mad. No doubt one solution would have been for the community collectively to have smaller families. But family planning was a nonexistent concept in those days, even for the unmarried. Years later, when a student of mine did a thesis in Barbados on women's attitudes toward pregnancy, I was struck by her finding that many of the pregnant unmarried women had sought to have a child, because so much of their psychological status was tied up in the business of giving birth, an activity that was clearly unrelated in their minds to being married.

My father said that no one ever talked to him about family planning, and he thought one had to be thankful for the number of children that the Lord sent, especially since He had a covenant with my father to provide for them. I found such an argument unpersuasive, but I could never get much further with him on it because he always stuck to his guns about his inherent ignorance of sexual matters when he was first married. He further accused me of never understanding the special agreements he had with the Almighty. It was a stalemate.

It was important, also, that our outdoor areas in the gap were not flat and boring. Mrs. Cobham at the entrance to the gap had ackee and mango trees that added spice to the outdoor life. Behind her was a small dugout area that quickly became a pond whenever the rainfall was significant. None of us dared swim there though, doubtless because the water in the pond was dark and frightening. In addition, a remarkable number of children in those days couldn't swim.

At the bottom of the gap were canes, which the older and stronger boys could uproot with their bare hands and taper with a pocket knife, then peel and cut into pieces they could chew to withdraw the sweet juice, spitting out the leftover mush and also avoiding the knots whose hardness could fracture a tooth. Mamma had coconut trees in the back that I never learned to climb, although I always wanted to, because it would have put me in a special group. But that was the kind of thing I never saw my father do, and Mamma never encouraged it either, because she didn't want to have me fall and break a limb.

By the time I was twelve years old, my friends and I were playing a lot of hopping-ball cricket in the gap, both inside and outside Alethaville's yard. Cricket with a hardball was obviously not allowed, not with little children around, some glass panes in windows, and villagers going to get water at the public standpipe on the main road. People had to live their lives, and a hardball was plainly dangerous. That no doubt accounted too for the first soccer I learned to play, which was with a hopping-ball the size of today's tennis ball. And since I was barefoot outdoors, the obvious trick was to learn how to manage that small ball without ripping up my toes on the rocks to be found everywhere in the gap, which in those years, as I have said, was simply never a paved road. I imitated every move I saw the island's top players perform at Kensington Oval when my father took my brothers and me there on Saturday afternoons.

I internalized the subtlety and finesse of Passion, the center-forward who played for Empire Club and whose nickname I thought nicely suited his style of play. I imagined myself growing up to play like him. Other clubs had good attackers, but not ones I dreamed of following. Besides, many of them had the habit of holding the ball too long. They needed a coach with authority to help them learn how to give up the ball before the opposition shut them down, which diluted their initial effectiveness at leaving their opponents going in the direction away from the ball because they had outrageously wrong-footed them with their delightful feints. But then they would proceed to give up their advantage by holding on to the ball until the opponents could recover and come at them in numbers. I never aspired to imitate Norville, the left-winger, because he had a left foot that no one else I knew could ever approximate. So I stuck faithfully to watching my man Passion and wondering whether the blue jersey and white shorts of Empire Club would fit me as snugly as Passion wore them. I went on later to wear the uniforms of high school and university teams, playing in attacking positions. But the teams' jerseys were never blue.

In the early 1950s, of course, an attacker could hit a goalkeeper and knock him with the ball over his goal line into the goal, which meant that to be a goalkeeper one had to be athletic and fearless like Merton Robinson or big and tall like Charles Alleyne. None of that was my cup of tea, small as I was. I also didn't take to that traditional way of defending, which required a fullback to kick the ball as hard as he could from in front of the goal area. For a ball equidistant between defender and an opponent, the defender had to rush headlong at that ball and "pull through," a Bajan expression that conveyed a heroic, partly suicidal mission. After all, it meant unflinchingly going after a ball with all one's strength while an opponent with the same idea in mind was coming from the opposite direction. Obviously an occasional ankle was broken or seriously bruised, which only heightened the drama and the heroics.

It was a long time before Barbados footballers recognized that defensive play of that type was silly, since clearing the ball like that meant your team lost possession and ultimate control of the ball. Since one couldn't score a goal without having possession of the ball, systematically giving it up was a poor strategy. All I can say is that defending like that and pulling through was a male thing. I still see flashes of it in Bajan football these days, particularly in the lower divisions where players haven't grasped the idea that soccer is a team sport, and individual heroics and intimidation tactics are a waste of time and effort. But some chaps are still compelled to frame their style of play in terms of pumping-iron contests, a framework long cast aside by all the top-level international teams. Passion's art and flair live on in my mind, as do the sessions with my father and brothers at Kensington Oval, which was the major sports arena of the day.

The emphasis on the outdoors, coupled with the relative safety of the neighborhood, encouraged all of us youngsters to make small side trips beyond the gap. That led me and some other friends one day to cross the Station Hill main road and venture down the small road that led to the entrance of the police commissioner's residence. I was surprised to find that the residence had its own tennis court, on which were playing two whites I'd never seen before. They were too young to be the commissioner, and they were surprisingly gentle and welcoming. Black children like me didn't cross paths much with white adults except teachers at school or clergy at church. So my expectations about these two tennis players were artificially constructed and not based on any substantive experience. The two tennis players were respectful, and my friends and I fetched the balls that they hit over the fence enclosing the court and stood watching a game we had never seen up close. None of our friends' schools or homes had a court. At the end of their game, they gave us a ball, and we skipped off home, because we had seen a part of Station Hill that was traditionally off the routine path. Despite the gentility of the players, I knew we didn't belong there, and the distance across the wire mesh between players and us spectators seemed vast. That is doubtless why I appreciated so much the players' pleasant disposition.

Sometimes we strolled through District A Station and went all the way to the back where the barracks were located and the off-duty officers slept. The police in those days were highly respected by us youngsters, with their sharp uniforms and broad leather belts, and their British way of saluting the officers with such military crispness. My father was good friends with several of the upper brass: One captain lived in Station Hill near to the prison; I knew another officer because I saw him at the seven o'clock Sunday night service at the Cathedral with his family; and my father took us several times to the home of yet another senior officer on bank holidays, and we ate and drank. His son played a calypso piano that caused me to move and wish I could age overnight so I could dance with the pretty adult damsels who were present but beyond my reach. It was on such occasions that I realized my father had extensive connections to friends in all sectors of Barbadian society, which didn't take away the feeling of peculiar strangeness I experienced when I was strolling down the entrance to the police commissioner's residence.

The outdoor life had a few drawbacks; one of its imposing requirements was that the children develop at least a cursory knowledge of the existing flora and the domestic animals kept in the village. To this day, I can't even identify with certainty the common bougainvillea. Neither my father nor Mamma had much interest in plants, although Mamma knew her vegetables like the back of her hand. It would be an understatement for me to say that I hated mixing with pigs and chickens and goats. My father and many other parents exacted a heavy price from us children, expecting us to care for animals we hated.

On that score, of course, there were other boys considerably more unlucky. Some youngsters had to get up early in the morning and march a pig off to a house located at a considerable distance from their own homes. The reason for this journey was never clear to me. Perhaps the boys were on their way to the home of the butcher who would slaughter the animal, or there was some other reason appreciated only by adults. The boys carrying out these chores were never skipping merrily along the road, embarked on an enterprise that brought contentment. There they were caught in a struggle with an undomesticated animal, hoping not to meet friends on the way, with the pig squealing and needing to be pushed or dragged or beaten into at least partial submission. Pigs in that situation always grasped the idea that they had some say about where they went. They understood that even though the owner or his proxy ultimately carried the day, pigs could still exact a heavy price for all the inconvenience. The more a poor boy dragged, the more noise the pig made while opposing the tension of the rope around its neck, and the more attention the whole affair attracted. This in turn prolonged things, much to the disgust of the boys who just wanted the struggle with the pig to be over. I am grateful I never had that ignominious experience. It did little for any young boy's personal esteem, and it underlined the meaning of poverty.

I can certainly find witnesses to testify that such experiences were good for us children. But that claim has never convinced me. I did not like the pigs and their filth, the pungent smell intensified by the Bajan climate, and the flies buzzing around that forced me to swipe at my face and ears three or four times a minute. I also did not like the idea that my parents were asleep in bed while we children cleaned up the sty. That must be why, as a boy, I learned the metaphor that was employed as an epithet to categorize as cruelly as possible someone's unpleasant behavior: "Boy, you behaving like a real boar hog." It was not, as foreigners might think, either an example of redundant speech or an attempt to refer specifically to the swine's uncastrated status. Rather, it was intended to bring to life the concentrated nature of one's contempt for the person's behavior that had been egregiously unpalatable. In the expression itself are at once the scent, the disarray, and the frank piggishness of the person. It should be obvious that a boar hog had to be worse than a bull in a china shop or a stampeding cow. The latter two expressions do not conflate sensations of smell, sight, and hearing as dramatically as the first one does.

So when one morning my father flogged me for not cleaning the pigsty effectively or properly or efficiently, it was a wasted exercise. No corporal punishment could teach me anything about cleaning up after pigs. I hold to my view that the Sunday morning flogging was gratuitous, although in the context of the Barbados of that era, I can understand it. That was a time when fathers insisted that their children, especially their sons, carry out chores with a pleasant disposition. A child's sucking of his teeth, known classically as a Bajan "chupse," when done in response to a parent's order to do something, could get a child into considerable trouble. It was the catalyst on that particular day. My father demanded that I accept a disagreeable task with a sunny outlook, that I curb my boyhood pride. I could not become a man before my time, nor exhibit traits of independence not yet welcomed by my own father. It was an immutable requirement that I accept the instruction with an even disposition to go clean up the stall. Unfortunately for me, it was not possible to clean up after a pig while smiling. And I believe my father had learned about the enforcement of rules from his own father, the Boss. So it was a Sunday morning of considerable unpleasantness for me.

The outdoor explorations that I mentioned earlier in the daily trips to elementary school at Saint Giles Boys' School up by the Ivy were manifest when I was seven and eight years old. Most of the time I walked to school, although my father drove me there at times. He rarely picked me up, though, which meant I walked back home with friends. That was a distance of a few miles, not considered far at the time. No bus made a direct connection from Station Hill to the Ivy, so to travel by bus would have required a trip into town and a change to a second bus. Besides, the walk was enjoyable, because we cut through other village areas and neighborhoods that we didn't know well or that we usually had little reason to enter.

Leaving home to go to school, I went down Station Hill and turned left through a small unpaved road—I think it was called Glendairy Road—that took me eventually fairly close to an external wall of Glendairy Prison, just before reaching Jacob's Ladder. As I remember it, the staircase was cut out of the rock, narrow enough so that no more than a little child and a parent could climb up side by side. The narrowness also permitted the children to hold on to the rock on the sides without falling. Who named this rock staircase and who built it remained a mystery to me. It facilitated, for walkers like myself, a shortcut between Station Hill and the Bridge Road area, which was a necessary intermediate passage before one could reach the tree-shaded area called Kingston.

In the mornings, it was imperative to keep an eye on the time, because tardiness was an offense punishable by a serious flogging at school and possibly at home again. So loitering without purpose was kept to a minimum in the morning, and we went quickly by the areas of Carrington Village and Welches. After strolling by Kingston, an area lined by recently built wall houses, we would then quickly cut through the grounds of the girls' school and reach the boys' playground.

The afternoon return trip had its delights. School was out then, and side trips were a mandatory part of the education. I avoided exiting the front of the school and turning left, which would have taken me to the Ivy in the direction of Tudor's Funeral Home. That was a village region unknown to me, even though a number of my school friends came from that direction. I've always wondered whether it was because I was afraid of Bottle-Neck, the man with the inconceivably long neck under that small head, who drove the only funeral carriage I knew of that was drawn by horses. His nickname was not intended to be disrespectful. It was just the only name by which we knew him. Furthermore, none of us schoolboys had given him that name. Bottle-Neck terrified all of us, without ever saying a single word to us boys or even throwing a glance in our direction, as he sat there high up, dressed all in black and driving a mysterious-looking carriage with who knows how many dead bodies inside. In my boyhood mind, his unusual appearance—with fixed unsmiling face and his characteristically rigid holding of the horses' reins—and connections to the dead made me wonder whether he was only partly alive, something like a walking duppie He inspired fear. So I stayed far from the Ivy neighborhood.

I usually departed the school ground through a gate that led directly to the girls' school. It was that gate that swung one day and just capsized me, causing a laceration on my forehead that frightened everybody for a short while and then left an ineffaceable scar just over my eye. Once I reached the front of the girls' school, I would exit onto the Kingston main road and proceed past an open space on the right with canes. Just as the canes ended, I would jump down onto a little track that led mysteriously into the inner workings of Flint Hall, an area where in my mind only white people or people who looked white lived, with their big dogs that barked and threatened me and my companions. We generally waited a few days before we would make that side trip again. We had to rebuild our reserves of energy and daring, because we all thought it possible that a dog might get loose and come beyond the confines of the residential grounds. Who knows what would have happened then?

There were two other places to which I walked regularly, usually accompanied by other brothers and sisters. The first was to afternoon Sunday school at Bank Hall Methodist Church, the one located squarely between those two hills on which people incessantly practiced their driving. They had to do it, because both hills were favorite testing sites of the police examiners. They used to make the candidates for the driver's license pull up on the steep hill, park, and then move off without rolling back, all in cars with clutch transmissions because there were few automatics then.

I attended Bank Hall Methodist Sunday School for years, even after I had been confirmed by the Anglicans. I don't know why my parents insisted so clearly that we attend it, especially since we all went to morning Sunday school at the Moravian Church on Roebuck Street. I suppose I had greater exposure to the Bible lessons and learning how to recite poems in public. I never really liked the dry Methodist hymns and the repetitive homilies of the school's leadership. But I loved the discussions after Sunday school with the senior boys and a few teachers. As I reached the early adolescent years of thirteen and fourteen, I also got to watch some of the older girls who wore high heels and had walks that turned the heads of the young boys like me and made us sigh with regret that we just weren't older, or maybe bigger, or perhaps just luckier.

The walk to Sunday school could be taken down Station Hill past the prison to Mrs. Alleyne's house—she often made baked macaroni and cheese for us on Sundays—and right through Powder Road, with the famous Powder House, whose function I never quite grasped. Its bizarre appearance suggested some former military or police activity. Or I could go through the road that took me behind the wall of District A. I didn't enjoy that route much, because it housed a little boy who couldn't speak. He lived in a house there, and he regularly threw small stones at people passing by and hassled other little children. I felt so sorry for him and wondered what I would do if his stone ever hit me.

The other place I walked to was the famous Bush Hall Yard. In those days the geographic marker was the windmill, which suggested that the area was originally the central yard of a sugarcane plantation. I went there to visit the Boss, and I would also stop by and see my father's sister, Aunt B—short for Blanche—whose house was about fifty yards away and who never struck me as much of a smiling aunt. These visits, which took place before June 1952 when the Boss died, constituted a very strange ritual. I had to make the trek with my brothers and sisters and without parental supervision. Both Bush Hall houses were dark and musty. Not odoriferous. Just smelling like the windows weren't opened very often, because no children lived there and the aging occupants had lost the energy necessary to keep the houses fresh and inviting. Barbadian windows that weren't opened regularly caused the house to take on the scent of uncirculated air. None of this may in fact have been true of these two houses. My recollection of the smells may simply have reflected my unwillingness to make these visits, coupled with the reality that those homes were unfamiliar to me. At the time, the Boss rarely spoke to me or anyone else; he was an old man sitting quietly in the corner of his upstairs bedroom, to whom I had to do homage and pay my respects. His reputation for strictness and the historic association of him and his cowskin made him a giant in my mind, although I never saw him strut or use his whip, or wheel his horse around and quicken the speed of his buggy. He would give me a few copper coins for having done my duty, and I never thought him stingy.

I must return to the subject of Aunt B's and the Boss's unsmiling visages. Try as my father did to explain it to me, I have never understood this habit that older Bajans still latch on to, this need to show a severe face to others, especially to children and to adults they don't know. These days I take some slightly pernicious pleasure in teasing the people to whom these seriously unpleasant faces belong. So I will not accept sitting in a taxi in Barbados while the driver insists on not smiling once during the entire trip. And I will ask relentlessly what is wrong and state that things cannot be as bad as the look on his face suggests. Or I will stand at the counter in the minimart in Saint Lawrence Gap with my money in my hand about to pay for what I have said that I wish to purchase, but not letting my money go. Not before the saleslady gives me a smile, I say. Then she lets it show, and it is clear that she is much more of a person with the smile than the gruff person who unsmilingly serves her clients. I assume Bajan pride made it clear in the colonial context that the smile was only for one's true intimates. Hence my image of the unsmiling adult face confronting a child with the expression, "You cyan be smiling with me because we en nuh friends." It was a way of reminding the child that laughter can make people not take us seriously. But at the same time, of course, the cold and unsmiling adult face inspires no hope of love and tolerance, which disorients the child. My father was often guilty, too, of this offense. Friends visiting my home for the first time would comment fearfully about my father's visage and wonder if they had committed a sin and were unwelcome in the future. I had to reassure them that my father was just like that. Of course, I experienced the same thing when I visited others and ran up against the coldness of the Bajan adult face, which always set me off wondering what I had done and whether I was welcome.

The transfer from Saint Giles to secondary school at Harrison College occurred when I was about eight and a half years old, some time around 1951. I quickly got the bicycle that had passed through the hands of my two older brothers. I persuaded Mamma to have it repainted a few years later by a man who worked at Cave Shepherd. He kept the bicycle a long time, like all the artisans of his day, making me wait for the finished product even though he had already received a deposit from my mother. Besides repainting it, with fancy double stripes on the bar and on the fenders, he put in at my request an odd-pedal, which made me one of the few youngsters in the whole island with a racing gear like the ones that Ken Farnum and all the competitive cyclists had. In other words, my back wheel couldn't spin without having the pedals turn. Racing cycles have long since given up that characteristic, particularly since a lot of competitive cycling these days is done on roads with hills, and it makes sense going down a hill to let your legs rest from the constant turning. My bicycle was very special to me, and it promptly opened up new vistas and radically transformed my life. This would not have happened without the concurrence of my father, for which I have always been grateful.

Having my own bicycle made me remarkably independent and led to the construction of a relationship between me and my cycle that transcended all others. I kept her well oiled and clean and tolerated no squeaking. Even when my senior sibling got a new Raleigh, I never felt the slightest pang of jealousy, because his new gift was a cycle with three speeds that made a lot of noise, ticking annoyingly all the time. My odd-pedal was quiet and turned with a hushing sound. With the help of other buddies, I learned how to make most simple repairs on her, and she was faithful. Only once did she act up, but it was not her fault entirely. I was riding through Bank Hall and was carrying a passenger on my bar, a buddy who had little experience with bikes. He didn't know that I often rode with casual fingers on the handles, something that aficionados knew instinctively. So suddenly, my passenger shifted his weight on the bar, something you don't do unless you're attentive to the position of the handle. Naturally, his changing position led to a realignment of the handle and the orientation of the bicycle. Both of us and my treasured cycle ended up in a gutter, a nasty gutter as we used to say, with filthy running water in it from which we believed we would catch ringworm, and all of this in front of laughing eyes in Bank Hall. My passenger deserved to walk after that, and I was not pleased either with my cycle, who should have known better than to respond to the sudden movement of an uninitiated, inexperienced passenger.

My cycle took me to school, to choir practice, to town to pick up vegetables that Mamma had bought. As I got older, I used my bicycle to travel to sing in the cemetery choir, to scout meetings, to the cinema, to visit a girlfriend or two, to the beach at Shot Hall or Brandons, to just about anyplace without having to wait for a bus or ask an adult for a lift in a car or on his bicycle. On bank holidays, I raced other friends to the airport in Christ Church or headed for Speightstown in Saint Peter.

The bicycle also permitted me the chance to canvass on behalf of my father when he decided in the early 1950s to seek a seat in the House of Assembly and represent the parish of Saint Michael. He had never asked me to do any such thing, but I thought it would be fun to talk to shopkeepers and the women sitting by their trays at locations like the Bridge Road corner and ask them to vote for him.

There was a woman who kept her tray just on the outside of the shop at the Bridge Road corner, and it was with her that I had the longest and best structured conversations. She was a dark-skinned, obese woman with a brassy mouth, bold and intemperate, the kind of woman I can see arriving at the pearly gates without the slightest fear.

She would greet Saint Peter with a loud explosion: "What de ass you tink you doing wid dis blasted door? Um in belong to you; open up, 'cause I arrive now and I come to see He. Tell He I heh."

Saint Peter, trembling a bit and taken off-guard by such directness, would send for the Master rather than face her. "The Master is coming," he would say.

"Tell He to stop comin' and come. I cyan wait heh all day. You look like you too foolish. You sure you know wuh yuh doin'? I en understan' how He cud put you heh to guard this blasted door. 'Cauz you en look like yuh got nuh sense."

But I faced her, taking every diluted insult she offered. And she had to dilute the coarseness of her words because I was but a boy. She had lots of personal pride, after all.

"I belong to de Labuh party, you hear? De party of workers, of black people. I votin' fuh Cox and Bryan. To hell with Griff an' dah white man he running 'bout wid."

She rejected my father and his white running mate with a long sibilant chupse that let me know there was a concentrated finality to her decision that only God Almighty could reverse.

"You tink we in de City? Dis is Saint Michael, an' Mottley cyan fool we up heh," she went on.

What she meant was that she lived and voted in Saint Michael, a parish that was both geographically and politically distinct from the city of Bridgetown, where Ernest Motley, a black man, was immensely popular with all the workers and convinced them to vote for him and against the Labor Party. She knew all too well that at the time there was a local vestry system that allowed Mr. Motley to do things directly for people, particularly in the urban area where he held sway. But everywhere else, black people had to vote Labor. The most interesting question flowing from all this was how did my father's alliance with the non-Labor party start? I assume it was through his connection to Mr. Motley. I wondered too whether the Boss's connection to plantation management ever played a role in my father's decision and made it possible for my father to think of these people as his friends or as individuals who might look out for him and his family.

These questions aren't easy to answer because political life is, of course, always more complicated than it appears at first blush. I learned that first lesson when my father taught me that in political strategic planning in those days, all the parties had spies in them who reported to the major financial interests in the country. After all, only a relatively small group of people on the island had a lot of money, and those people were almost always white. Those interests had to be protected regardless of which political party was in power. So my father may have seen it as simpler and more direct to ally with the Conservatives.

Nevertheless, when my father left in 1954 for New York and it wasn't clear whether he was returning soon, his creditors all came down on Mamma with a vengeance. The party stalwarts, those who stood up in political meetings with him and slapped his back in solidarity, all disappeared, and so every loophole was closed. Mamma cried first, then gritted her teeth and decided to rely on her wits, supported by her children, her friends in Station Hill, and her God. It was something to see her operate, once she got going. In later years, my father never quite understood why she was so suspicious of individuals who asserted their friendship for him in a public fashion. But I knew where she had developed this mistrust and I could sense at those times her longing for the simplicity and directness of Miss Garner and Daisy Best.

Eventually, the Bridge Road woman and I became friends after a fashion, and I would hail her as Coxie as I passed by on my bike and reminded her of her preference for Mencea Cox the candidate. She felt that the Conservatives were too closely and obviously aligned with the upper class and they would leave her in the lurch once the going got rough. It was a simplistic argument, because even the so-called parties of the lower classes needed an alliance with moneyed interests. These logic-based arguments provided little consolation for Mamma, who felt betrayed by my father's friends. She didn't think it amusing when people tried to take bread out the mouths of her six children. And at that time, she found herself able to cope because my father was as constant and dependable as the registered letters that came from him in New York with mathematical regularity.

Sometimes I would pick up the letters at the post office in town and sign for them, since my face was readily identifiable as a Griffith. I would get on my bicycle and ride home, knowing I had the money in my pocket that would take care of us for another week. But my father's decision to eschew an alliance with the Labor Party has been a source of puzzlement for me, and I have regretted not discussing this issue with him, especially since I know he had no trouble with Labor Party principles.

Alethaville remained remarkably ordered and functional once we all got past the original trauma of his leaving. Little changed in the drawing room, which still housed his desk where he kept all his receipts pierced by a metal arrow, which meant they were all there but in no organized fashion. There was the bookcase with the glass front, with which I had a love-hate relationship. I loved books and liked browsing through that bookcase, which housed my favorite texts that I had at home. On the other hand, I had been partly responsible once for fracturing the glass on that bookcase as I played on the neighboring rocking chair, which I rode mercilessly as a stationary bicycle, expert enough that I could keep it balanced on just one of its rockers and could then make it spin a full circle. So what if I would lose my equilibrium occasionally and go crashing toward the bookcase with a glass front? My father and Mamma had this silly idea that drawing rooms were meant for sedate behavior, which, after all, could only be embraced by sedentary adults, not by athletic young boys whose imagination could easily see the possibilities inherent in any piece of furniture to enhance their interests in running and jumping.

The drawing room was a rectangular space of quite ample size, since it also contained a piano on which my father vamped from time to time. Next to the old-time settee with a bottom made of cane was an ancient Victrola that I cannot recall ever having heard working. On it was placed the newer phonograph that came from the United States with records of Bing Crosby and Gene Autry and somebody else playing "Do the Huckle Buck." That music was bizarrely far from our world, but some relative had sent it expecting the gift to be appreciated.

There was a narrow corridor we called the passage that connected the drawing room to the dining room at the back of the house. In the passage was the telephone hung on a wall, a location that was private enough and still accessible to all the neighbors who would use it for emergencies, even once in the middle of the night for a woman who was very seriously ill and whose husband was at his wit's end. The dining room was easily the most used room in the house. That was where neighbors would drop in and hold court. It was where Mamma or Daisy would settle to pick the rice, because in those days everybody would pick rice before washing and cooking it. In the picking, extraneous matter was removed, including discolored grains and bugs. The dining room table was also where serious table tennis matches were played. All the rooms in Alethaville, except for my parents' bedroom, served multiple functions.

Nothing changed the activity so radically at Alethaville as the pouring, insistent rain. Not the usual ephemeral showers that lasted a half-hour, but the rain that went on for hours and darkened the whole neighborhood, causing windows and doors to be shut in the middle of the day, and disrupting everybody's schedule. Since just about no one had a car, few of us went to school when it rained like that; getting to work was a major problem, since reaching a bus stop on the main road required a walk of at least a hundred yards. In the blistering rain, that was an unworkable project, because your clothes would be totally soaked within the first ten yards of your venturing outside. Walking in the rain like that never conjured up any visions of strolling in the Paris rain. Nobody considered it romantic, especially since it was a well-established village belief that if one got wet, a cold wasn't far behind.

What I liked most about that kind of rain and the semi-darkness it produced was the dramatic effect it had on the day's cuisine at Alethaville. The usual lunch was out, and Daisy and Mamma set about to make bakes. I can easily imagine that under such conditions in the days long preceding my time, with caregivers unable to circulate easily and do their shopping on the main roads proximate to the villages, the mothers and wives decided to make do with what they had on hand at home. Hence they resorted to making bakes. A bake was something I can only say reminds me of what I came to understand later was a form of pancake, although our bakes smelled nothing like a pancake. Furthermore, the pancakes I came to know later up North in America were devoid of the sacred association that I linked to bakes. Proust can have his madeleine. I had Bajan bakes.

Mamma fried her bakes in hot, hot oil, which Barbadians know is hotter than simply hot oil. I can't cook, but cooking friends tell me that a bake was made from batter that consisted of flour, nutmeg, sugar, salt for flavor, butter, and water. The nutmeg was grated and mixed in a tot—a tin-cup of varying sizes made by local tin smiths—with sugar, salt, and a few drops of vanilla essence. The frying pan had to be preheated with lard oil before the bake batter was dropped in. But hot (although some people like their bakes cold) and fresh and all fried up, the bake was supported by an ambience that couldn't be created else-where, with the rain pounding on the galvanized paling roof and only a little light coming in from the outside. Some lucky youngsters had their bakes with "cocoa tea" or regular "green tea." The bake was set in royal relief against a piece of ham or a fried egg, although the less affluent had to be contented with plain bakes and tea, or perhaps a soupçon of salt-fish, what the calypsonian Sparrow would later call bacalao, although he was referring to more than just saltfish. For those lucky enough to have an egg with their bakes, the task recognized by every child I knew was to eat the bakes and make the egg last long, long, long, which is longer than just long. And one wanted to taste the damned egg, but the logi-cal order of things was murderous in that circumstance. If you touched that egg too soon, it was hard to hold yourself back. The more you ate, the less you had, reflecting a principle of mathematics invented by some cruel adult. The more egg you ate, the less remained on the plate. On the other hand, you couldn't just leave the egg there, sitting by itself all unappreciated and getting cold and dry. So I plunged eventually and internalized the harsh lesson that the best of pleasure eventually must end. Worst of all, time came when as an adult, I eventually lost my taste for bakes. Not so much that I rejected bakes, but I couldn't surround the bakes with the semi-darkness and the sound of rain hitting the galva-nized roof and the reassuring presence of adults and the bustling of Mamma and Daisy Best in the kitchen. Eating bakes outside of Alethaville made no sense.

One time in 1955, the rain started, and it poured for hours. The wind came too. Those who had electricity had it knocked out in no time. The white manager of Rediffusion came on the air himself, with his unhurried articulation and British accent, early in the morning, wak-ing up everybody, telling us all it was serious business. It was a hurricane. Roofs flew off left and right; electricity poles were uprooted and fell over like little matchsticks; wooden houses slid off their makeshift founda-tions. The pond on Mrs. Cobham's land filled up and extended itself, cutting off the shortcut passage from our gap to the area behind us. But Alethaville didn't budge. She held firm and even provided shelter to some neighbors. In the weeks after, when the storm had subsided and people were looking to rebuild and repair, many from the gap and the surrounding area went to the local government in town and asked for help. Then my father's name appeared to mean something, because the officials told everybody to go get some kind of attestation from somebody at Alethaville, once they heard the name was Griffith, swearing that the individuals had in fact lost things in the hurricane. My eldest brother wrote most of the letters. But the helpful magic was in the name my father had left behind, even though he was away from the island.

It brought to mind the idea, better appreciated in later years, that my father had contributed much to turning Alethaville into a safe place for us. It is clear he had substantial help from Mamma and from the broader community and even from the whole generation. I recall only one episode when I experienced real fear. That was the night I turned into the gap and heard a man running behind me. I turned and saw, vague in the moonlit night, the face of a white man on foot who was clearly intent on doing harm. I took off, abandoning my cherished cycle, and sprinted the sixty yards or so to the protection of Alethaville. My father couldn't figure out what had happened, because I could hardly talk. My second older brother couldn't say much either, because he had been in front of me when he realized that I was running, obviously horror-stricken. So he took off too. My father didn't hesitate. He went straight to District A and reported the matter. In minutes, the police apprehended a man who lived in the area and bore a strange name whose origin I never knew. It turned out that he was after a youngster who had teased him and then turned into the gap before Junior and I had done so. In those days, it was easy for the police to believe the man's version of the story and that he had never intended to cause harm to me or my brother. It would have been unthinkable to make an attack on us and get away with it. At that time of night and with the nature of gap life the way it was, the man could not have reasonably intended anything criminal, not against anybody who lived at Alethaville. In fact, despite the explicit extent of our real fear, everybody just poked fun at us, and the matter entered the family lore of life at Alethaville.

The only other time I remember that people spoke seriously of the police and of the courts was the time that a young woman in the gap got into a struggle with her boyfriend and she stabbed him with a knife. But that was a domestic dispute, with the victim and perpetrator identified and with no member of the community ever in any danger. Furthermore, that action did not disturb the other hallowed customs of the gap. For example, it was a nightly ritual for women to return from their church services, and as they entered the gap, they would start saying goodnight to anyone they encountered, sometimes even to people they couldn't see but who they imagined were not yet asleep because a telltale light was still on. Between nine o'clock and nine-thirty on a Wednesday night, when many of the Protestant churches had finished their midweek service, you could hear the women walking up the gap, shoes hitting little unseen stones in the dark.

"Goodnight, Mrs. Cobham; Goodnight, Mrs. Holder; Goodnight, Mrs. Griff, I going in."

"How was the service tonight?"

"Real sweet. But da man cyan preach at all, you know. Real cold pone."

"Well, at least you said your prayers tonight."

"Dah is true, yuh know. And yuh hav to gih God thanks."

"Sweetheart, guh long and get some rest fuh dem bones."

Now I hear many of the churches have eliminated these night services, and there are gangs circulating in certain neighborhoods, and people are afraid.

The doors of Alethaville were locked only after the last person came in at night. No one thought seriously that the locks were meant to keep any enterprising person out. People were kept out by the old-fashioned moral notion that crime against neighbors was wrong. Additionally, there was the practical idea that somebody in the gap would be sure to see any interloper. Pulling off a crime without being identified was a near impossibility. Being identified would bring such shame and scorn upon your family! So in fact, if one intended to steal, it would have to be done outside one's own village, which would create a host of other problems. That is no doubt why in those days certain laws, like loitering with intent to steal, could make such sense to us. What would a young man from Station Hill be doing up in the Ivy at two o'clock in the morning? The possibilities were simple and self-evident: visiting a girlfriend, which was easily verified by the police; coming from a party—in the middle of the week? The police didn't have to work very hard to prove their point. If you lived in Station Hill, that's where you belonged late at night, unless you were sowing wild oats with a woman, which was always permissible, but rarely done like that if you had to work the next day and you knew you didn't have a bicycle for transportation. The conclusion then was easy for any magistrate, and with the full support of all the people up in Station Hill. It was impossible to loiter, in a community not your own and late at night, without having a guilty mind and intent. Such utter elegant simplicity of yesteryear's logic!

Alethaville stood up to the pressures created by my father's decision to go abroad in 1954. We followed in 1956, torn between the established pleasures of Alethaville and the sung praises of a New York with streets presumed to be paved in gold. I know many people in Station Hill envied us, because we all had heard the same stories of glory up North. I have always thought that my father could have told us the true story or a more realistic one. Certainly Mamma needed to know that the adaptation was potentially easier for youth. Maybe none of us would have believed the truth, because the myths about New York were more seductive and romantically heroic, reinforced by the examples of West Indians who returned to Barbados from New York to visit relatives. The Bajan New Yorkers always seemed to be sharply dressed, because they wore styles and colors to which Bajans left behind had no access. The returning visitors also flaunted a foreign accent that made them appear special, and they walked in that hurried New York fashion. They spent money in a way we didn't understand, talking about tips and always recognizing that whatever you did for them deserved a monetary reward. This reinforced our primitive ideas that money was just more plentiful in New York than in Barbados. It would be some years before I understood just how hard West Indian immigrants actually worked up North. Fortunately, it did not take me quite as long to fill the void caused by leaving my odd-pedal bicycle in Barbados.

CHAPTER SIX

Transplantation

They wandered in the wilderness in a solitary way ... Hungry and thirsty, their soul fainted in them. Then they cried unto the Lord in their trouble, and he delivered them.

Psalm 107:4-6

It all seemed so peculiar, so unexpected. My father met us at the New York airport, and a man I did not know was driving the car that took my brother and me to Brooklyn. My father had no automobile of his own. So the chauffeur, a member of my father's church, had been kind enough to allow my father use of his car to pick us up. It might have been easier on my nerves if I had known the driver of the car. Not knowing him added more to the strangeness of the situation. As this unknown chauffeur maneuvered his car smoothly through the streets, which were unfamiliar to me and partly shrouded by the haze of a night in spring, I tried pointlessly to get my bearings and to see whether I could predict the next turn the car would make. The encounter with a father I had not seen in about two years was not so celebratory as I had imagined it would be. He looked the same, and I was glad to have him back. But the unusualness of the surroundings diluted the joyfulness of the reunion. Our conversation was halting. No raucously merry welcoming committee. My father seemed tense, as though he needed to readapt to this role of being directly responsible for children who were older and a bit wiser than they were when he had last seen them. And the chauffeur remained respectfully quiet, focused on this task he had to carry out before hurrying home to his own family and preparing for the work rituals of the next day. His silence amplified his presence, and he seemed to take up more space in the car than just the driver's seat.

I was in disarray and unable to focus my attention, because of all that was so new around me, so novel to my unsophisticated, Barbadian senses. I was unsettled by the slowly dawning realization that I had never been with my father in an automobile that he was not driving. Seeing him settled in a passenger's seat suggested there was something wrong with him. Beyond my adolescent comprehension was the simple fact that he did not own the car and that he had not yet reached the financial status to lay claim to car ownership in this new country. So this big, wide, shiny mechanical wonder, with more lights on its dashboard than I had ever seen, did not belong to my father. This monstrous vehicle, which was about as imposing as the one used by the governor of Barbados, was owned by one of my father's friends.

I was not only disconcerted by the driver and the car and the wide streets with the streetlights that regulated traffic so effortlessly. I was put off by the chilly spring evening air in May 1956 that was like no ambient temperature I had ever felt in Barbados. I was uncomfortably dressed in a pair of long pants and a jacket that constituted a suit I'd not yet gotten accustomed to wearing and that I didn't think fitted me very well. That is what most boys say about their first suit when they have worn short pants all their lives. This transition from short pants to long pants was hard enough for boys growing up in the Caribbean, particularly because the first pair of long pants rarely fit well, except in the case of boys who were very tall. This clothing transition was significantly more complex when it appeared in the midst of these major geographic and migration moves.

Besides, there was no shooting of stars when the plane touched down on the tarmac. No orchestra opened up with a striking song of welcome. The arrival was plain and ordinary and, yes, strange. I wondered fleetingly why I had left Barbados to come to this, a New York that sparked no great thrills. None at all. My own feelings were at odds with the fact that my father felt so proud of his accomplishment in beginning the move of the family to the United States.

I had been told there would be gold in the streets. But there was none, insofar as I could see with the headlights of a car. The few trees I sighted had no dollar bills fluttering from them, despite what folklore had spread down in Barbados about life in New York. Certainly nothing to that point compensated for leaving a host of friends, both boys and girls, and a climate that faithfully supported the constant use of my bicycle and enhanced my freedom and independence. That is why I have developed suspicion of newspaper stories touting the excitement of immigrant arrivals in New York, unless the immigrants are really running from something. They can't possibly be as confident about what they're running toward as those stories always claim. I knew I hadn't run from anything in Barbados, not from sun and sea and Daisy, and certainly not from my bicycle.

Things got no better when we arrived at Lewis Avenue in Brooklyn where my father had rented a small apartment so we could settle in to this new life. I assumed he did his best in finding the apartment, although it would be many years before I understood fully what it really took to rent an apartment, put furniture in it, stock the refrigerator with food and drink, turn on the telephone, find a television set, put sheets on the bed and cutlery in the kitchen. I would eventually appreciate that it took money, energy, time, and even some ingenuity.

When I first saw the apartment, it seemed clean and neat enough, with linoleum that covered every floor and gave an antiseptic look and feel to every room. However, its structural organization made no functional sense. It was not like Alethaville, where the kitchen was proximate to the dining room; bedrooms were auspiciously separate so that privacy was an obvious objective in the building of the house; and the drawing room was clearly designated as the formal place for receiving visitors. The Lewis Avenue apartment may in its original construction have made sense. But by the time we moved in, it was no more than a group of rooms cobbled together with no attention to the activities of a family. There was no relationship between kitchen and dining room. No passageway for one to move from front to back without going through someone's bedroom. The apartment was also located in no-man's-land as far as I was concerned. There was not a single friend within walking distance, not even my father's friends. In fact, people didn't walk anywhere. They all rushed to take a bus or a subway, an action even to this day I could never term walking. We used to walk to Bridgetown from Alethaville, and from Station Hill to Bank Hall, saying good morning or hello respectfully to people, checking on the health of friends, monitoring the angular tilt of a particular "bumbum" wending its way on about its owner's business. That was walking. People didn't walk in Brooklyn. Especially not in winter, with the wind and the cold whipping round their legs and making their poor lips turn white and crack.

How could one honestly say that a Bajan could walk in Brooklyn when he had to be poking his hands in those heavy coats, bundling up, and keeping track of which pocket he kept his lip balm in, constantly pulling it across those chapped lips to tone down the pain. Then too, he had to keep track of house keys, a few of them, because there was always more than one door to open to get into wherever he was living. As I learned later, that is why the West Indians had to be provided a special West Indian Day at the end of the summer, so they could hear their calypso music and walk about the place or stand up liming and engaging in bare shittalk. Once a year, all New York got to see what it was to walk Bajan style.

I was surprised to learn that my father wasn't a friend of the people who lived in the apartment below us. I had never before contemplated the possibility of not being friends with my neighbors when all of us lived in a relatively circumscribed building that housed four or five apartments. The occupants of one apartment had a dog that barked ferociously every time I walked by, and I was convinced that one day the dog would come running out and attack me. It was a hard introduction to life in Brooklyn, and as a consequence, no simple matter to comprehend my father's decision to leave the coral rock for this. How could we share a building with other people and not talk to them, not go next door and borrow salt or pepper or sit down and have a drink and tell jokes or argue about some local political event?

I wished that the neighbors understood how things worked in Barbados, that they cooked with the same spices that Mamma always used. So I thought it would be logical to talk to them, at the time when the odor emanating from baking meat was sneaking under our apartment door.

"Man, yuh look as though yuh cooking up a storm!"

"Yeh, man. I turning my han'. I know yuh smell de peppers an' ting." The neighbor would have got the hint as well as appreciated the compliment.

"Here, man. Taste dis pork chop. Tell me wuh yuh think."

"Man, it taste good, yuh know. You kin cook. It only need a lil bit more pepper. De nex' time yuh mekkin' up yuh ingreasements, call me so I kin show yuh how much pepper muh mother usually put in."

With that imaginary conversation taking place between the occupants of proximate apartments, we would have participated in the ritual of neighbors, and I might have had a pork chop and spent a few minutes in conversation with people who shared the collective building space. However, that didn't happen in Brooklyn. It wasn't Station Hill or Road View.

Mamma had not come with us, so my father made some very convoluted arrangements to ensure that his sons would eat a hot meal while he was away at work. Not surprisingly, the plan was set up with the famous Aunt Dais, the woman who inspired fear long before I actually met her in the flesh and who had been for years the invisible owner of Alethaville, invisible to me because she had left Barbados before I was born. We met that first night of my arrival, because convention dictated that I pay my respects to her, and waiting too long would certainly have been viewed as a cultural offense.

Daisy Taitt was not a particularly big woman, not tall, and certainly not stout, as Barbadians would have said back home. Besides the slight accumulation of fat around her abdomen, there was no excess weight to be found anywhere. She was a moderately brown-skinned woman who generally wore a wig when she went out, something that was a common practice in those days among Bajans in Brooklyn. It was as much a sign of middle-class status as it was a suggestion that the wearer of the wig was not pleased with the appearance of her natural hair. Aunt Dais was most fussy with her appearance on Sundays when she went to church or when she attended some church function, like the annual flower day ceremony at a neighboring church. That is when her fur coat came out or her fur stole was elegantly draped around her shoulders.

As I quickly found out, she was always on the move, constantly involved in one activity or another, clearly a woman of action who had a plan for every minute of the day. She, too, had forgotten how to walk Bajan style, but her forgetting had been purposeful, deliberate, and intentional. There were certain Bajan habits she was proud to have given up, and walking with indolence was one of them. She thought such a habit translated into habitual laziness, a preoccupation with sloth. She didn't like this business of wasting time or taking an hour to do something when five minutes or so would suffice. That would be "frigging spider for half the increase," something she had clearly sworn off. Every time I saw her rushing off somewhere, I could hear my old headmaster's injunction singing in my ears: "Go to the ant, thou sluggard; consider her ways and be wise." Or his alternative plea, which he uttered when exasperated by the laziness of his students: "How long wilt thou sleep, O sluggard?" These verses from the Biblical Proverbs were doubtless sustained reference points for Aunt Dais, who was determined to be productive with every ounce of energy available in her body.

Decades later, when she returned to Barbados to live, she would ask me on many occasions how Bajans on the island, her island, could take so much time to do so little. She was frustrated just watching people cleaning up the space in front of their houses. The sweeper would move the broom a few times but then stop to speak to someone or just look up to check the color of the clouds in the sky.

"Mrs. Taitt, the sky setting up above, you know. I think it gine rain."

"Don't say dat. I put some clothes 'pon de line early dis morning, an' deh have to dry."

"Wuh, you think de Lord up deh thinking 'bout you clothes? He busying 'bout de crops. We need de rainwater."

"Don't say dat. I promise to visit old Miss Clark up in Welches. She sick, yuh know."

"Dah is a different thing. But de Lord still gine provide for she. De Lord does move in He own mysterious way. And you cyan let nuh rain stop you from doing He will."

Clearly this would lengthen the period of time taken to complete the uncomplicated task of sweeping. Aunt Dais would scratch her head and utter that characteristic sucking sound of a Bajan chupse and conclude that the island was going soft and heading for perdition. She had forgotten how to walk, how to lime.

On the other hand, I recognized that she had not just given up liming and strolling Bajan style. She had also renounced other classic Bajan traits, because she had decided that those traits, companions of a too relaxed style of living, did not facilitate her achieving what she had set out to accomplish by staying in New York and putting up with the grinding winter. Bajans of her generation wanted to improve their socioeconomic position and "mek something of demselves," something that could only be achieved by those who had learned how "to turn round fast," or "how to turn deh hand." This wasn't about spinning around quickly but about moving with determination, keeping one's objectives clear, and harnessing energy in the service of reaching the objectives.

Some of her friends called her Daisy; most of them called her Aunt Dais; a few, like her doctor, called her Mrs. Taitt. Her pastor at the well-known Saint Philip's Episcopal Church, where she gave so generously of her time, called her Mrs. Taitt too. My father called her Aunt Dais, and I followed suit. But come to think of it, I saw the two of them together on very few occasions, partly because both of them worked long hours during the week, and then on weekends they went to different churches. She rarely sat—by that I mean sitting still and not doing anything else—and held an interactive conversation with me, one where we talked to each other freely. I always had the feeling that she talked and talked and gave her opinion and talked some more and I was supposed to listen. That was when she was in a good mood. If she was upset, she didn't care whether I listened. She just kept up her soliloquies while moving even faster than usual, as she carried out her chores.

"I gave that man my hard-earned money, you hear? I tell him I would be home in the morning fixing my house, and he could pass by then to repair the fridge. He promise me he would come. Now he just call me and say he can't make it. And what am I supposed to do? That ent fair. I have to go and clean Mrs. Schwartz's house this afternoon. I can't wait here for that man. My lady depending on me, and I can't let she down. I can't do that. So I don't understand how that man could just up and leave me stranded like that. And how he expect to make a living doing that to people?"

The appeals were made to no one in particular. Aunt Dais worked hard and she believed in treating people fairly. She also thought that workers like herself should always have an ethics base to undergird their behavior. When someone paid you to do a job, fairness demanded its completion at the agreed time.

The difference in our ages was substantial, since she was the sister of Mamma's mother. And by Bajan tradition, there would be no topic on which she was less expert than I, except in the domain of some technical subject that I would have learned at school. She was not, I'm sure my father would agree, given to easy laughter, which made her face stay harsher than she sometimes intended. That persuaded some of us, put in Bajan terms, that she "wasn't nuh sweetbread," which suggested a clear potential for irritability under the right circumstances. I am being fair in stating that she had also forgotten how to laugh, at least in the deep, free Bajan sort of way. She certainly did not cackle out or belly-laugh at anybody's joke, not even in private. This may not all have been her fault, since it was a long Bajan tradition that the adults of her generation not smile much and not appear to be warm, particularly toward children. So she did not routinely kiss or hug me, although she did it when we first met.

She lived on Herkimer Street, which was a two-bus distance away from Lewis Avenue and required a bothersome transfer. The street itself was lined by brownstones on both sides, marvelous residences that had clearly seen grander days. Not that Aunt Dais and all the other Barbadians on that street didn't keep their houses in immaculate fashion. They certainly did. But most of them had resorted to a new way of using these brownstones.

The street-level floor was often assigned to serve as a drawing room, dining room, and kitchen. Instead of going up the steps, or the stoop as the Americans called it, from the street, I walked straight ahead and found a metal door on the side of the steps that led to the street-floor residence. The floor above, the first floor proper, was where they slept. Then the rooms on the other floors were rented out to a host of single blacks who were trying to make it in New York. Some of those rooms had cooking facilities, and others did not. But those roomers, who obviously helped their landlords to pay the mortgages on the buildings, were alternately seen as a blessing and a curse. Roomers brought in rental income. They also came with their own unique personalities and cultural practices that were sometimes at odds with the values of the owners. This led some zealous proprietors to institute rules that were intended to constrict the lives of the poor roomers in certain aspects. Aunt Dais didn't tolerate overnight visitors to her roomers, and no one was allowed to make much noise, which meant to many roomers that they were not permitted to give any sign of life, to laugh, or to have a vibrant discussion. I was always struck by the unearthly quietness in these brownstones on this particular section of Herkimer Street. It is true that the bustling intersection of Nostrand Avenue and Fulton Street was just around the corner. But that bustle of living, produced by both blacks and whites at this time in the '50s, did not penetrate the walls of the Bajan houses on Herkimer Street.

The architect who designed those buildings had never contemplated what light meant to young boys from Barbados. There were windows on the back and front of Aunt Dais's brownstone, and since each side was connected to another building, it meant that all the hallways were dark and mysterious and characterized by the heavy presence of mahogany stairs. No doubt the construction conserved heat in the winter, but it also clearly kept the outside separated from the building's interior. As an adult, I managed to see the remodeled interior of brownstones like these that a single family lived in, where rooms ran without interruption from the back to the front of the building. This gave light a chance to enter and play on the contents of the room, accentuating the high ceilings, the artistic woodwork, the molding that dated from an era when artisans had time to ply their trade. But that architectural possibility got no serious consideration on Herkimer Street. And for Aunt Dais, it would have meant a significant reduction in income to transform her home into a place all meant for a single family.

As I said, my father was at work. He never had the time for any discussion about what it felt like to take two buses from Lewis Avenue to Herkimer Street in the middle of the day to pick up a hot meal and return with it to the apartment, so he and my oldest brother could eat it later when they returned home. Since it was summertime, I had not entered school yet and I was the natural choice for this chore. But I didn't like it, not realizing of course that it was just the kind of adaptation that immigrants had to make in order to live in the new city. The accomplishment of this task required me to have a key to Aunt Dais's house, since she usually left for work before I arrived to pick up the food. I had first to open the metal door on the street level. Then would come the two wooden doors, both heavy and seemingly impenetrable to all life, air, and light, before I would make it into the living quarters. She had no children and also no domestic animals to give the place an air of being lived in. Indeed, I rarely had a conversation with anyone in that house outside the kitchen.

Sometimes I would sit in the living room on the couch that had been carefully covered in plastic, a habit that Bajans passed on faithfully to each other in New York and one that I always wondered whether expatriates in Toronto and London copied. Those plastic-covered chairs were supposed to last forever and to resist an onslaught from children. The plastic was also a protection from substances the chairs and couches rarely encountered, since few Bajans lived in those drawing rooms.

Seated in that sedate living room, I would spend time quietly thinking about what I had left behind. I never had the courage to turn on the television or the Grundig radio and record player that sat on the floor and was about hip level. I could not bring myself to turn on any of these devices, because they never had the appearance of being used. The Grundig high-fidelity set was especially frightening. Aunt Dais kept an embroidered dust protector on it. And the German manufacturer set the white buttons so adroitly against a faux-mahogany casing that I was awed by the apparent grandness of the machine. So the house remained silent, and so did I. When I had grown tired of the quiet and the solitude, I would pick up the carrier, that multilevel contraption that kept the meat and sauce separated from the vegetables and the rice, and go to catch the two buses for the return trip. Sometimes there would be a whole apple pie that had come from Mr. Taitt, Aunt Dais's husband, who for years drove a minitruck that belonged to the company that made those pies.

Wanting to connect to people and to New York meant I had to take matters into my own hands. Before leaving Barbados, two friends had given me addresses. The pen pal of a buddy who sang in the choir with me was located in Brooklyn on DeKalb Avenue; the other was a Manhattan address. In both cases I estimated independently where I thought I would find these people and I started out. Looking for the Brooklyn address, I just walked, finally hitting the number after about an hour or so. The adults in the family were nonplussed that I just showed up, although the young boy I was looking for seemed to take the whole thing in stride. He was getting dressed to go to a meeting of his scout troop, and we talked for a while before he had to go off. I never saw him again.

The Manhattan address was more complicated. I chose a subway stop arbitrarily, got off there, found the avenue I wanted and then started searching for the right number. An hour later, I rang the doorbell of the apartment and delivered the greetings I had brought from Barbados. There was a look in the eyes of the middle-aged women I had gone to see that asked what a fourteen-year-old boy like me was doing so far from home by himself. I ignored the unstated comment. I didn't know enough to be afraid or worried about anything. After exchanging a few pleasantries, I went back to Brooklyn and Lewis Avenue, to the loneliness that was so hard for me to verbalize. All the Bajans around me took it for granted that one was better off in New York. But that was not so obvious to me as it was to them. It was in the scheme of things that Barbadians who had the opportunity to immigrate to New York would as a matter of course make the journey. However, it was to me questionable that many children happy in their native countries would vote to support their parents' decision in this matter.

My father's thoughtfulness about education led him quickly enough to take me and an older brother to meet the authorities at Boys High School, so that it could be determined what grade level we would enter in September when the autumn term started. My father had also already explored with my oldest sibling, who had preceded me to New York, what the university situation was like. I suspected that Elwin was a bit surprised by the complexity of his arrangements and by the expectation that he would have to take the financial responsibility for his education so quickly and so early. But my own grasp of that was likely colored by my father's insistence that a primary objective of the massive upheaval and transplantation of our family was to obtain for us children better advanced education than we could obtain in Barbados. A part of his argumentation was founded on the reality that in the 1950s, I would have had to go overseas to obtain a bachelor's degree. Discounting Codrington College in Barbados, which was exclusively for the training of Anglican priests, the closest West Indian university was located in Jamaica. Everyone knew that New York City offered university education through well-known places like City College and Brooklyn College. What my father's argument always seemed to brush off so glibly was the importance of the family and the broader community in supporting the young person's quest. He was persuaded that the major parental task was to set up the expectation of the child's obtaining a university education. Once that was done, then the child was expected to follow through and just complete the required studies.

My father may, of course, have suggested that my synopsis of his position was unjust. He may also have rightly pointed out at the time that his hands were full. There were six children to care for, and he was working very hard. The other point made regularly by parents of his generation was that many others had achieved solidly, had become professionals in disparate disciplines. So all any child had to do was to take hold of the opportunities encountered in this new American environment. No handholding by parents was necessary. The trouble was that such a position essentially argued that all children were alike. Their abilities and needs didn't differ, so differential sensitivity from the parents, especially from West Indian parents, was not called for.

I met with the authorities at Boys High and was lucky enough to grasp instinctively what my father expected me to do and to sense his natural inclination not to hold my hand. It was never a negative feeling or a communication between us of any hostility. It was just the way it was. He would be there if something major happened. He'd never let another student or a teacher mistreat me. But the job of learning was my area of responsibility. He gave me no advice when I decided to take civics and elementary algebra in school that first summer. I concluded quickly that it would make sense to get a head start on the work, and I knew that school would be a reasonable way to get out of the apartment, see some of New York, and if lucky, meet some new friends. It was self-evident that he and Aunt Dais and Mr. Taitt and any grown-up Bajan I met would approve my taking summer classes. School was always good, especially if it cost no one any money.

It turned out that the civics class was taught by a man who didn't want to be there, and he had obviously concluded that none of his students wished to be there either. Not that his conclusion was entirely wrong. Some of the students came late, others missed several days; a few looked as though they had just got out of bed and wished to be left alone. On the other hand, I was genuinely interested in New York and life in America and wanted to hear how local governments worked. I tried to engage him with my quiet attentiveness and he plodded on with his view that everyone in the class was a moron. I wondered whether there was some plot to punish me and all the other students, since registering for that class required that particular teacher to work. The man was by any measure an incompetent teacher. But his lack of competence was most malignant when it translated into his view that his students had no minds deserving of any cultivation.

The algebra was an easy A. In contrast with the civics instructor, the mathematics teacher gave frequent quizzes and clear examinations; he was energetic and wanted his students to do well. It was easy for me to respond because I had nothing else with which to clutter up my mind. When I left class, I didn't rush home to be with friends or even to watch television. I didn't find Amos and Andy very funny, and most of the shows reflected a culture that held relatively little interest for me. So I concentrated on the schoolwork.

Once after class, a Chinese boy invited me to go with him to play table tennis. He took me to Chinatown, and we went into an athletic club where he had obviously been before. I enjoyed that excursion, and I held my own on the table, even against all the spin he sent at me with his unusual way of holding the racquet. The other secret pleasure I had was to descend into a subway station and buy an O'Henry or a Baby Ruth chocolate bar for five cents from a machine. It was pure magic to see a chocolate bar with nuts just come popping out of a machine. No such machines existed in Barbados. And chocolate bars for that price did not drop out of a machine accessible to children. But such pleasure did not last forever. After all, how long could a small bar like that last in the hands of a young boy? I would be a full-fledged adult before I would have the chance to compare an O'Henry to the chocolate made by Parisian chocolatiers. Then I would resent the fact that the Americans had taken advantage of my ignorance for so many years.

Every immigrant must have a list of first experiences that have been etched into consciousness, that defy obliteration, and that have both public and private meanings. The first Sunday at Saint Leonard's was another of those firsts. Saint Leonard's was my father's church, the one that had been so instrumental in making it possible for him to stay in the United States.

At the time, there were many Bajans attending Saint Leonard's, with some other West Indians and a few Americans, although I suspected that if one questioned the Americans closely, their backgrounds would reveal a linkage to West Indians somewhere in the past. Some Bajans there had gone to Canada first and then made the trip across; they would make fun of my comments about the cold because Montreal's cold was the real thing. Other Bajans had made the trip first to Panama and then connected to New York. The direct route was also quite common. But all these people gathered to inspect the Reverend's newly arrived sons. Because it was one way of cultivating their goodwill, my father allowed them the privilege of carrying out their review, of giving advice, of commenting in their sanctimonious way about any and everything concerning his family. On the other hand, it is possible that they usurped the privilege as congregations often do when it concerns their pastors. Many churchgoers still believe that their pastors, and by extension the pastors' families, belong to the faithful of the church. This means that pastors and their families have no inherent right to privacy, a principle that has always offended me.

Most of my father's parishioners seemed old or much older than I was, and they had long ceased being able to talk to children, which is of course what children habitually say about adults with whom they have had little previous connection. Some of them wanted to be liked and to be seen as kind and gracious. But all this review would take place again once Mamma and the girls arrived some months later. The parishioners were not intentionally malicious. However, their tendency to pry ran afoul of my natural aversion to public scrutiny in churches. I have never enjoyed standing up and having a church full of people go over me with searching eyes. I do not like it now, and I did not enjoy it then. I have never bothered with the argument about how were the church members supposed to know I was there and that I was a new member and so on. My father pointed out, and reasonably so, that protocol required they meet his children. So much for protocol. I still did not like the practice.

St. Leonard's became the symbol of regimentation for me. I had to join the choir, since my father had already talked so much about my experience in choirs back home. I sang alto because my treble voice had cracked by then, and I sat next to a group of women who had been singing long before I was born and who marveled that I could really point a psalm without getting anxious. They meant well and did a good job with the tools they had, although they never could quite get accustomed to the shrilly tone of some of the sopranos in front of them. Still, for years I was impressed by the members' attempt to be faithful in their commitment to the choir, especially when I realized that many of them were doing their best to re-create a church choir atmosphere that they had left in Barbados many years before. It was evident, for example, when the choir sang Stainer's "Crucifixion" on Good Friday. The tenor and bass took on the solos with a surprisingly good technique and a tone that made clear they had sung elsewhere before, when they were younger, and they had a memory of excellence ringing in their ears. A couple of years later, I would sing the tenor solos too and admire the choir members even more.

However, the regimentation was still there. When my father got the idea to start a Bible class that met after the already long morning service, I had to be there, a mandatory sign-in. I can't possibly be the first preacher's son to walk the face of the Brooklyn earth. But I just couldn't establish a connection with many of his parishioners. I had particular trouble with those who had brought with them their Bajan values that had lost a lot of their import in this new culture but that they insisted on retaining. They were the parishioners who didn't smile, who worked hard not to give a compliment, but who also insisted on being treated like my grandparents. Not everybody was like this. Some of them loved to laugh and urged me to do well at whatever I wanted. Some went out of their way to be kind and indulging.

St. Leonard's was a study in contradiction and in contrasts. I had once read a short history of the birth of the African-American Orthodox Church in the United States, which is the denomination to which Saint Leonard's belonged. I know there was another church in Florida and one located in Harlem. A bishop told me about the apostolic connection between the African-American Orthodox Church and the Catholic See. It was important to him, because he was always intent on making clear the theological correctness of this church to which I know he had made a significant contribution. In addition, he wanted no questioning of the legitimacy of those he had elevated to the priesthood. That was no doubt another way of saying that he wanted no suspicions about his own consecration. The bishop was a good friend of my father, and that prelate was likely the first scholar in Brooklyn to open my eyes gently to the distinction between blacks and whites in the United States. As I grasped it, the existence of the African-American Orthodox Church was a symbolic rebellion of blacks against white control of the Episcopal and Anglican churches. Those latter denominations had taken their time in recognizing the potential of blacks to participate in the ordained leadership of the church.

It was also this bishop who told my father about that special bookstore that was located in Harlem, the one with books about black people all throughout the Diaspora. I had to do a term paper on some subject having to do with the American Civil War, and my father took me there. The owner of the store reached up to a shelf, took a book down, and let me have it. He made it clear that he would be helpful to any youngster who understood the inherent value of a book. He drove home his point that he expected me to make use of the book. I had not known that my father had these connections to blacks in New York who were interested in the intellectual life. I grasped the fact more readily later when one night he took me to a play at an Episcopal church in Harlem. That was the night I met a writer named Langston Hughes, who smiled and shook my hand. It was not a momentous occasion, because my ignorance could not make it so. At least it was a moment, one facilitated by my own father.

With all this, Saint Leonard's was a Bajan church through and through. Its form of service was decidedly Anglican, although the bells and the incense made it a high church. It took time for me to become accustomed to the rituals, since Saint Michael's Cathedral in Barbados where I had grown up had consistently been low church. The building that Saint Leonard's occupied in 1956 had been recently bought from a group of Jews who, I always assumed, left the neighborhood of Putnam Avenue when the racial mix made them uncomfortable. The edifice was imposing and stood out from the residential buildings around it. It had a magnificent chancel, and even a fairly substantial upstairs section at the back of the church that would be filled up on days when there was some special service going on. Saint Leonard's possessed a definitive majesty that challenged those Bajans who liked looking down their noses at any church that wasn't directly linked to the Archbishop of Canterbury. While Saint Leonard's represented a kind of upstart Anglicanism, it was hard to get past the impressiveness of the building's structure. In other words, this was no storefront church. The church also had a first-class organ that, when awakened by the likes of Bert Rudder, the assistant organist at the time, caused many a visiting Bajan to decide that Saint Leonard's was a real church after all. That's how they would put it to me: "Man, da is a real church, yuh know." That would be said in a conspiratorial and knowing way, underlining the speaker's unstated idea that, yes, there were indeed some real and some fake churches.

Of course, most of the doubters changed their minds once they heard my father preach. He knew, as did everybody else in the church and outside the church, that he could preach. Some people said that he could handle himself in the pulpit. Others framed it differently:

"The Reverend knows his Bible and can explain it."

One man told me: "Boy, your father can talk. He has a way with the Word."

It was evident that my father had his own following in Saint Leonard's. I never asked the rector, his boss after all, what he thought about my father's preaching. I certainly never talked to him about his view of my father within the context of the organization, whose politics I only partly grasped then but in retrospect can understand much better. My father tried too hard to convince me that churches were run by or with the grace of God, and without knowing quite why, I found it impossible to follow his line of reasoning. I maintained then that men were men, and a church was an organization like any other. My conclusions were justified by the tension that erupted publicly from time to time between him and the rector.

Once Mamma and the others joined us, it was evident that the Lewis Avenue apartment was too small. But through contacts with Bajans my father had known for a very long time in some church or other, he managed to rent a three-bedroom walk-up on the third floor of a building on New York Avenue just off Eastern Parkway. In the mid-'50s, that area was a community that was undergoing change. The Jews were still there in abundance, and their older generation sat on the benches of Eastern Parkway and talked in accents and languages I could not understand. At least they used the benches, which stayed repaired and usable. Years later, when the Jews were all gone, the benches fell into disrepair, and I could never tell which version of the story was true: black people tore up the benches or the authorities stopped repairing them.

The people who sat on those benches were all white at the time we first moved there. I noticed their unusual way of dressing, with long dark coats and hats and beards. The names of the doctors that appeared on the signs in front of so many of the houses on both sides of Eastern Parkway appeared foreign. Then I saw similar names on the stores located on Nostrand Avenue, which ran parallel to New York Avenue, and I heard about kosher for the first time in my life. Well, that is not exactly so, since I had been an attentive student of the Old Testament. It was true that I had never seen in Barbados any stores dealing in kosher products, and I had certainly not met anyone who insisted on eating that way. It was indeed a Jewish community that stretched in all four directions from our new residence, but the West Indians were moving in with a vengeance. Still, for the three years I stayed there before going off to the university, the community was best described as an integrated one, although it was only twice that I saw the inside of any of the homes in which white people lived in that community, and not the ones who happened to occupy the buildings on our block.

My father must have known that moving to New York Avenue would be better for Mamma than staying on Lewis Avenue. The neighborhood was clearly friendlier in appearance. When the weather was good, she could walk straight down New York Avenue to see her Aunt Dais on Herkimer Street. She could also go to Nostrand Avenue to shop; she learned to navigate the A&P Store and to purchase her chickens and eggs from a Jewish merchant who respected the way she examined the merchandise and looked out for her children. The three youngest children could also find their way unescorted back toward Crown Street where their elementary school was located. Our Bajan dentist who served us was also a relatively short walk away from our apartment.

I toyed with the question of whether my father had ever really talked to Mamma about moving the family from Barbados to Brooklyn and the process by which he would accomplish it. He was in Brooklyn two years before we all joined him. In that time when he was separated from the rest of the family, he developed ways of dealing with the uniquely American world around him. I believe it was very hard for him to have walked away from all that belonged to him in Barbados: the friends, the contacts, the achievements, and the recognition. It had to have been very difficult to start again in New York and to rebuild. I can only guess at what the pressure was like to have influenced him to leave in the first place. Two years later came the decision that we should join him in Brooklyn. My father never told me explicitly that he had discussed the decision with Mamma and concluded that it was the right time to have us join him.

In the course of our professions, my father and I have talked to many families over the years who made the same decision about emigration of their families. The results of the transplantation have varied. That very year I arrived in New York, I met several West Indian families who had made the same trip, and the sons were with me at Boys High School. So there is nothing new or surprising about my own father's decision. But of interest was whether he had contemplated the advantages and the inconveniences of the decision before it was taken; whether they discussed the kinds of adaptations that would be necessary for all the family members concerned to minimize the stress that was inherent in the move.

Back home in Barbados, my father gave his sermons and, particularly since he was not officially in charge of a church and he also had other interests and work, Mamma could stay at home or go to other services as she wished. In Brooklyn, my father expected both her and us to attend Saint Leonard's faithfully, which was convenient for him but not for us all the time. Keeping up with the styles in the church wasn't easy for a woman taking care of her six children. Also, for the first time, she had no help in the kitchen, no Daisy Best to start cleaning the meat, no tropical sounds to keep her company, and the space was restricted. She had to be careful about speaking too loudly, and Mrs. Holder and Miss Garner were not there as familiar supports. Even to go and visit Aunt Dais, she had practically to make an appointment. She couldn't just drop in, because after all, Aunt Dais had her own life and her own work and her own house to take care of. But he would not have told Mamma that she would encounter any of that.

I believe that had we offered to a hundred Bajans the option of migrating to New York in 1956, a majority of them would have accepted the offer, so strong was the pull of the stories about what that American city had to give. However, the hype about New York City was not realized. I could not believe that everybody, young and old, educationally prepared or not, sick or well, could adjust with equal success to the burdensome task of living as a new immigrant. It couldn't possibly happen. New York is full of those who have been worn out just by the winter alone. It can be a city that tears unabashedly and with vindictiveness at the unprepared who cannot meet the city on her terms. Mamma was among the unprepared, something my father suspected, although he may not have wished to acknowledge it.

Even he, with his sophistication and experience in New York, was sometimes at a loss as to how to confront the city's ways. For example, I told him one day about the school's requirement that I present a certificate showing that I had had a dental examination. He winced, because his shoulders were sagging from the already established debt. It was out of the question to pay a dentist to see me. A teacher who liked me found a neighborhood clinic that would examine my teeth and provide the required attestation. We got out of that mess, because I was able to describe our predicament to a supportive and understanding adult. But it remained a powerful example to me of what a new city can do to its immigrants. Of course, authorities would have argued that the requirements of a dental examination promoted both individual and community health, a point that I would readily concede. However, those same authorities never contemplated the unintended impact of their public health regulation on immigrants without significant resources. In short, the rule heightened the level of our family's stress, a lot of which was borne by Mamma.

CHAPTER SEVEN

Las' Train at the Gayheart

> *Praise him with the timbrel and dance ...*
> *Praise him upon the loud cymbals ...*
>
> Psalm 150:4-5

In September, I found my way to Boys High School, and a new life started. On the very first day, I met Roy. He had migrated with his family about the same time that we had. He used to live on the other side of Station Hill, going toward Hothersal Turning, which accounts for my not knowing him very well. But we fast became good friends, which is something you do when you're looking for comfort in a strange environment. He introduced me to Hugh, who was another new arrival. We enlarged the group with a Haitian, a Trinidadian, and a Saint Lucian. But the mainstay was three Bajans and the Trinidadian. We joined the soccer team, although I think it more accurate to state that we took it over, and we started going everywhere together, even on weekends. The only problem was that we belonged to different churches, which we solved from time to time by going to special services in a group at one particular church. For that exercise, I recall the only person excluded was the Trinidadian, who took his Catholicism seriously. The others went anywhere, which was a habit to which I had become accustomed in Barbados. What I particularly liked about the group was our adherence to values we all shared. We hated violence; we understood that school was a serious and necessary phase of our lives; we treated our elders with unstinting respect, which included all our teachers; we loved music; and we were attracted to girls, something that our West Indian backgrounds had naturally enhanced.

Our preference for these values also made it easy for us to stick together and exclude the intrusions coming from other directions. So not one of us ever had an interest in the gang culture that existed in certain areas of Brooklyn's Bedford-Stuyvesant at that time. We just didn't understand those boys and neither did my father, Mamma, or any of the other adults we encountered on weekends. Drugs existed in our minds as a mythical concept, although we occasionally saw men on Fulton Street swaying effortlessly in the wind without ever falling down, and we knew that such artistic standing could only be accomplished with the help of drugs. There was never any haughtiness in our rejection of those substances. We had to concede that in all our islands rum had wreaked havoc with a segment of the population.

I believe that a large number of Barbadian immigrants to New York lived in crowded circumstances: small apartments, large families, or at least in situations that permitted relatively little privacy. It was an important adaptive technique to find a place to spend time away from where one slept. Boys High School opened up early. Some of us went to the gym, where there was top-flight basketball being played. But that excluded me because I had never played that game before. In addition, at a place like Boys, no place existed for diminutive players, unless they were possessed of remarkable talent that could fend off the aggressive drive of the big basketballers. So I stayed out of the gym in the early morning and, with a number of other friends who were non-basketballers, we occupied a space in the corridor just outside the gym and sang and played music. It was akin to singing in our bathroom; the walls enhanced everything we did and convinced us we emitted marvelous sound. This was a time when lots of youngsters loved imitating the many groups making it big on the radio. In addition, a number of us liked drumming on the chairs and providing a special rhythm background for some of the calypsos and boleros we sang.

After I'd had enough of the music, I would go to a chemistry laboratory to help the teacher set up the classroom for that day's experiments. I was one of his student assistants, and I cannot recall who referred me for the position. But I know that I'd been told it was important to have on my school record credits for volunteer service, since colleges would consider that as carefully as my academic performance. This teacher was one of those wonderfully peculiar instructors who took his profession seriously. After obtaining his college degree, he had accepted an officer's commission in a branch of the armed services. As he once told it to me, he decided to leave the service when one day a superior officer walked into his office for a chat about some issue. My teacher looked up, and the other officer was indicating to him that he should stand. My teacher was not the type to tolerate such pointless indignities. He explained to me that he and his superior were in a private setting, so invoking the ritual was not meant to protect good order in the organization; it was simply intended to humiliate. With that kind of experience under his belt, he resigned his commission.

Over several years, we talked about everything under the sun. He believed in the dialogue between teacher and student as a way of clarifying the student's ideas and solidifying the student's values. He was the first teacher I met who evinced no special interest in God. On the other hand, he was a fanatic about following concepts of fairness and equitable access to privilege. He thought there was much to learn from the lines in the student cafeteria downstairs. The queues were often lengthy, and boys would think up all sorts of strategies that afforded them the chance to skip to the head of the line so as to be served first. My teacher was offended by such unfairness, and he had no qualms about speaking out against the practice that other teachers had of signing passes that would permit some of their students to jump to the head of the queue. During these many months of our exchanges, he accumulated a substantial amount of information about me, which he distilled into a special letter that he forwarded to colleges when the time came for me to apply. It was his clear position that teachers who wrote sloppy letters of recommendation ought to be ashamed of themselves. The letter of reference was an important tool in the life of every student, and teachers should employ it judiciously for the benefit of the student. He wondered what a teacher was there for, if not to be helpful to his charges, particularly since in my case I needed help in understanding how to negotiate the American system of education so as to maximize my chances of success.

Finally, we talked about race relations in the United States, and he had little tolerance for all the discussion and the posturing from both blacks and whites. He admitted he was a white man, and he knew I was a black student. But he couldn't understand what skin color had to do with anything about the worth of human beings. It was clear he thought his superior in the military was an ass, and that man was white. He also thought the black students who occasionally disrupted the chemistry classes were asses, and they were black. So what? A time came in my teacher's life when an ass was an ass, and it didn't have anything to do with color. He promised me that if I took school seriously, he'd write me the kind of letter that would help me gain admission to one of the finest colleges in the nation. He was a white man making that promise to a black student, and color didn't have a thing to do with it. I followed his advice, and he kept his promise.

My father generally found it hard to grant that individuals like my teacher could have a functional and constructive center to their lives that was not rooted in God. Nevertheless, I remained in awe of that particular teacher because of his commitment to fairness and to the unsullied development of the youngsters in his charge. He always kept his word, and he despised the exploitation of one person by another. I do not know how he might have resolved major political problems at the international level. But I do know he believed that honesty and impartiality would help him resolve most differences at the personal level. I expect my father would still ask, with the chuckle that usually translated his recognition of having cornered me in an argument, what was to become of my teacher's soul. I cannot answer that. But if a letter of reference from me will help that teacher when he encounters Saint Peter at the pearly gates, then I will write with the greatest enthusiasm.

One of the important elements about Boys High at that time was the existence of teachers on its staff who served as magnets for certain groups of boys. Several of the coaches served that function, of course. But one of the science teachers, a black man with a Caribbean background, allowed himself to be used like that by my group of West Indians. I have no idea how it started, although it could not have been during the fall soccer season, since we left school immediately then to head for the athletic fields that were several miles away from the school itself. One day I just found my group in his classroom chatting. He was in fact never a science teacher of mine. But after school, while he prepared for the next day's lessons and wrote homework assignments on the board, this group of boys held discussions with him and with each other. It was clear we did not want to head home to what were relatively dreary apartments in the winter. So he kept us focused on ideas, on talk, on thinking, and in a context that was protective and safe. He was one of the patient teachers in that school at the time, and without advertising it, he provided strategic support for a group of us who wanted to lean on him, but in our own way.

There were rarely any discussions of a religious nature with this teacher, which caused me to frame in my mind the repeated questions about whether one could be decent and fair and respectful of others without being rooted in religion. With a definitive single-mindedness, my father harped on one's relationship with God as a major justification for doing good and doing right. These two teachers I have mentioned seemed to have some other basis for their moral compass, a possibility that my father was not willing to consider, although he couldn't make it disappear. These teachers were unusual in my adolescent world.

Boys High School occupied a lot of my time in those days, and one of my favorite activities was participating as a member of the soccer team that was a wonderful haven for so many of the boys who had come in from other countries. Haiti, Barbados, Trinidad, Saint Lucia, Guadeloupe, Grand Cayman, Italy, and Hungary were some of the countries represented on the team. I enjoyed the center forward position and the experience of playing in full uniforms in games that were well organized, with referees and all the accoutrements of officialdom. I had not done that in Barbados before I left.

In those days, there were intramural games at Harrison College for my age group. But no one had a proper uniform, and no boy my age had football boots. Still, in Brooklyn, the boys from the Caribbean stood out, and it was obvious that we had handled the ball before, since our skills were quite good. Our team won its share of games, and a group of us became known throughout the school as the guys on the soccer team, as players of a sport not quite understood in a school that was known citywide for its runners and its basketball players. But we had still won some respect in a school that had high esteem for its athletes.

It was therefore not an easy thing for me to accept getting hurt on the field. I remember going for a ball that was loose and bouncing. My opponent got there first and kicked the ball with the intent of clearing it from his end of the field. It was not a gentle pass, but a clearance kick. The ball flew straight up and caught me in the face, in the eye, in the right eye. The ball had laces in those days, and I always imagined that the lace had gone into my eye. The accident was so unusual that I had to believe all the circumstances of this freak incident were themselves bizarre. I had been in lots of plays where opponents were seeking to hurt me. Not so that the damage would be permanent, but with an intent to cause me pain, so that I would be intimidated and would therefore play with less confidence. But this particular opponent had not been especially aggressive. He just kicked hard. Once hit in the face, I bent over with my hands going up in reflex fashion, as though to protect myself from the next blow that obviously was not coming, since I was in no fight with anybody.

When I straightened up and took my hands away, I realized I could not see out of one eye. Other players around me said later that they had been frightened by the sight of a string of blood dangling from my right eye. The coach took me to the nearest hospital that specialized in eye diseases, and the examination revealed significant internal bleeding, enough to prevent me from seeing with that eye. They sent me home that night with instructions to return the next day. My father took me back for the reexamination, and I was glad he was there. The decision was made to hospitalize me, to cover both my eyes and repeatedly check the pressure in my right eye. I assumed they were monitoring me medically, with the possibility always there that surgery might be needed. My father kept vigil faithfully, coming everyday to talk to a young son flat on his back who was wondering whether he was about to lose the vision in one eye.

Those ten days were among the most directly traumatic of my life to that date. The doctors and nurses, not all but most of them, hadn't a clue about how to treat a young boy immobilized for the first time in his life from a soccer injury. I am not referring to the eye injury itself, which they understood quite well, but to the business of managing a young boy who was terrified. Every day, of course, the doctors came, took the bandages off my eyes, and proceeded to measure the pressure in my injured eye. The procedure required me to hold my eyelids open while they brought this small machine down on my eyeball and determined the eye pressure. As I looked straight up, I could see the machine descending slowly toward my eyeball. I always had the feeling that the machine would not stop but would penetrate my eye and land somewhere in my brain. I couldn't hold my eyes still. Instead of trying to calm me down, the doctors would resort to threats. So my eyelids would flicker increasingly, and the physicians would become more irritated. I was taking more time than they wanted to spend at my bedside. It was an exercise in mutual frustration. They thought me a difficult patient, and I found them a group of insensitive professionals who needed retraining in the business of caring for people. Certainly they knew little or nothing about caring for children. They just wouldn't talk to me about what I thought was important. After all, it was my eye, my vision, and I was an athlete at the time. I wanted to know whether I would see out of that eye again, whether I would play soccer during the next season. The doctors just didn't understand that my eye was part of me, and an impaired eye could interfere with my private dreams. Years later I would understand why consumers of health care became so vociferous and demanded that doctors listen to them.

Some of the nurses didn't have time for me either. They didn't readily grasp the idea that my bandaged eyes meant that I was functionally blind for those ten days of hospitalization. Furthermore, I was under strict orders not to leave the bed, which forced me to carry out all activities in bed and to be fed by nursing staff or by my father. After I used the straw in the soup, my father was patient enough to rinse the straw before he put it in the milk. Some nurses found that extra step too burdensome, and I would almost gag at the taste of mixed-up soup and milk. I had to be washed in bed, something that some nurses understood as a potential violation of one's privacy. But others thought of it as just another act they had to perform before they went home. I would grit my teeth and suffer the indignity of being a patient, a role I would understand in later years that young health care professionals needed some time to appreciate fully.

After ten days in the hospital, on my back with both eyes shut down, suffering the indignities that the permanently blind must endure day in and day out, the bandages came off. I assume the bleeding had stopped, and the pressure in the eye had returned to normal, because the doctors decided I could return home. But I had to stay in the house for another six weeks or so. The vision in that eye gradually returned, and eventually I got back to school. The return wasn't as smooth as I had hoped. I found it difficult to recapture some of my study habits, particularly the confidence in my memory that had served me so well to that time. I especially disliked the news that all of a sudden my presence at sports activities was not welcome. The coach who was in charge of soccer was nervous when I was around him. Of course, I knew that he liked me. However, his anxiety was palpable, and I assumed that he considered himself responsible for what had happened to my eye. He thought that I had some sort of academic promise and had the potential to amount to something. He didn't want any accidents compromising my vision, not on his watch. I never played soccer for that school anymore, but I did take it up again once I got to the university.

Of this experience, this episode of being forced to lie quietly in bed for many days, with both eyes bandaged and effectively sightless, I can still see my father acting as a nurse. This was not a role that he had played often in my life. He had not been there as the nurse, carrying out that important caring function, when in Barbados before we all emigrated I had caught the dreaded yellow jaundice. It was also not he who propped me up in bed so that I could breathe more easily the night I had whooping cough. It was my mother who had been the nurse on those occasions. However, my father took to the role in Brooklyn and tended me dutifully. I was not in any position then to lament how the mighty had fallen. Adolescent children, fifteen-year-olds, have nothing mighty about them. But the proposition of possibly losing sight in one eye was legitimately frightening. In that sense, there was something tragic about the idea of moving from the status of having two eyes to having vision in only one. That would have been a mighty fall, and it was profoundly comforting to have my father there.

I did reasonably well academically and got moved to the scholarship track in the school, to sit amid a group of boys who were primarily white and who were headed to college with apparently no questions asked. That is to say that both their teachers and their parents had agreed without formally stating it that these boys were going on to the next step. I remember them well, because they walked with assurance and had the best student volunteer assignments locked up among them. It was fun being in those classes, because the teachers treated these students differently. The instructors talked to them as they would talk to their own sons or at least to people they cared about, and the boys were constantly being pushed to be curious about the world around them. There was something well defined about this world of which they spoke. I didn't have any well-formulated objections to where I was being directed. I followed, recognizing only that it was not a world I knew.

For example, one English teacher, who made it clear he liked me and wanted to peer into my world of Barbadians in Brooklyn, kept a narrow blackboard in his classroom on which he pinned all the reviews of Broadway plays that were printed in the major magazines and daily newspapers. What surprised me even more was that he kept up a dialogue about Broadway and theater with one particular boy in the class who saw every play once it opened to the public. Now the other students weren't excluded from the conversation. It was more like an unstated game, and to play, one had to read at least the reviews if not see the plays. I did not have a strong liking for theater, and I did not take easily to the analysis of dramatic literature. But I did like language, and I eventually appreciated that teacher's comment that he thought I ought to consider writing essays. He never told me then what he saw in my writing. He just made the comment and went on about his business, as though he didn't want to seem too forward and overstep his bounds with someone like me, whom I think he had trouble understanding. This particular teacher introduced me to Walt Whitman and others. But my favorite at that time turned out to be Robert Frost, whose lines fitted my sense of rhythm and appealed to my practical view of the world.

My biggest connection came to my next teacher of English, a man who I decided was far ahead of his time and who was interested in the pure pleasure of intellectual inquiry and exchange. He welcomed us, closed the doors to his classroom, and forced us just to think and talk. But we had to be honest and do the assigned reading. There was no room in his class for shirking duty to one's own brain; one must feed it. I recall well the discussion of Richard Wright that he forged, which led me to explore Wright on my own. He made us examine Iago and Desdemona from every possible angle. This was long before the advent of African-American studies. Only another two or three black students were in this class of about twenty-five, and he was a white teacher. He believed in intellectual openness, and it was clear he lived the ideal that both blacks and whites could think well once their minds were cultivated to do so. He wanted me to write creatively, too, and he especially urged me to read critically. It was because of this white instructor's aggressive teaching style that I encountered the Harlem Renaissance. It was he who first introduced me to the notion of black esthetics.

I know my father would recall my coming home and telling him that another teacher and guidance adviser had suggested that I apply for a place at a special international scholarship camp, which took place in the summer near Rhinebeck in upstate New York. The teachers raved about this camp, because it was run by a foundation that brought together boys from many different countries as well as from different communities in the United States. I was lucky to win a spot at the camp, which required no unusual outlay of money from my father. The places at camp were awarded without reference to the family's ability to pay. The leadership of the camp did want to talk to all the campers' parents before the start of the summer season. So I set up an appointment with them to meet my father and Mamma on a particular Friday night and told them both about it. The night came, and two gentlemen rang the bell to the apartment. I went downstairs and had to tell them that neither one of my parents was at home. They looked at me in disbelief, because they rightly thought that they had set up an appointment in a thoughtful fashion and well in advance. I did not expect Mamma to be there. She did not usually handle family business with outsiders. My father had taken on that role. So I wondered how my father had managed to convince himself that it was reasonable not to show up for the appointment. I never said anything to him about his missing that meeting. I have always assumed that he simply had to work. But then, why not say so specifically and clearly? Perhaps some other reason caused him to stay away, one that demanded his silence. It was an inexplicable moment of confusion and embarrassment.

Nevertheless, the camp leadership did not withdraw my invitation to attend the camp. The camp itself was an unusual experience for a boy who had been in the United States just over a year. It was indeed unique, and I had the chance then to talk to boys my age about countries and cultures I had never thought about. It was hard enough learning from the other Americans, many of whom had culinary habits with which I was distinctly unfamiliar. Their parents often sent what they called "care packages," which turned out to be parcels of cookies and candy and meats like bologna and salami that I had never tasted. I could barely stand the smell of the bologna and salami, and once, when I decided I would be open and taste them, I couldn't believe that people ate such bland food. I started praying for an angel to pass over the tent with some Bajan pepper-sauce so that I could spice up these foreign meats. It was an important introduction to what many of the boys at camp, especially those from New York City, apparently ate every day at home. I was stunned. And so I had to explain to them how Mamma would never serve any meat or even fish that smelled like meat or fish. That was a concept they had never heard of. They argued that meat was supposed to smell like meat, and fish like fish, an idea that was anathema to Mamma. I explained to them how all meat and fish in our house went through the process of being washed in lime and salt overnight, then rinsed, then left to marinate in a concoction of spices that, as Mamma described it, "cut the raw smell of the meat or fish."

I am reminded now of being on a plane with a Bajan colleague on the way to participate in a project on behalf of the University of the West Indies. The stewardess came by and served the meal to both of us. My colleague was uncertain of whether the meat on the tray actually looked like the chicken it was advertised to be. She eyed it suspiciously, then looked around her cagily before she brought the tray up to her nose and smelled it. I burst out laughing and thought immediately of Mamma, who always subjected food to the ultimate test of what it smelled like. She had certain scents that were off limits in her kitchen. Besides fish and chicken, her other major offender was eggs, particularly when used in cakes and desserts. Any pastry, for example, that conveyed the smell of raw eggs was banished forever. Of course, such bias was sure to influence her children, and I concede that I just couldn't eat the salami and bologna being offered so graciously to me in that camp tent, especially since the summer temperature probably enhanced the meaty smell of the products.

There were other things to learn, despite my obvious inability to come to terms with the foreign meats. Many of the campers were gifted musicians, and that was my first experience of having violins and cellos and violas and the classical guitar all being played right around me, and by youngsters, not adults. Even in my arena of singing, I was amazed one day when, in the middle of an outdoor rehearsal, the music counselor turned to a camper and asked for a note because he thought the group was going flat. He had turned to that particular camper because the camper had perfect pitch, a phenomenon I had not encountered before. It opened my eyes to the potential breadth of interests that young boys could have, and their skills were at a level of excellence I had not imagined possible for youth of my age.

I had to sit up and take stock when I realized that, for someone like me who was already in love with things linguistic, there was one boy at this camp who was already a published poet. For some inexplicable reason, I had never tried my hand at writing poems, even though I had memorized a good number of sonnets and other love poems that had attracted me. But I had never contemplated laying out my thoughts in that form. I was not even sure that I could tackle certain subjects that I traditionally kept to myself. So writing a poem would force me to take risks and intellectual chances that I was not yet ready to assume.

The camp was organized in such a way as to encourage the boys to experiment with leadership concepts. Several of each day's activities were set up with boys leading them, including groups that kept the camp clean and that took care of the preparation of daily meals. The leadership of these activities was not carried out well by all the camper-leaders. But at least we had the chance to try out our skills at managing people and to learn from our mistakes. I did not perform brilliantly when my turn came. However, I started to come to terms with the feelings evoked by the experience of taking a group in hand and planning a coordinated response to a particular problem. It was the beginning of a long-term excursion into measuring my abilities against those of other group members and confronting the crucial idea that, although I had different strengths and weaknesses from those of the other boys, I could still do well and perform my required tasks creditably.

The experience also set me to reflecting seriously on my own cultural background and to thinking about what difference between people actually meant in practical terms. For example, the camp pushed other sports but made it decidedly clear that basketball was not a revered activity at camp. Some silly explanation was offered by camp leaders that basketball promoted too much competition among the boys. Or perhaps they said it made for the wrong type of competition. I termed the explanation silly because I don't believe a single boy thought it to be a truthful accounting. There was no doubt in any of our minds that somebody in the camp's leadership group didn't like basketball. That was clear. What we were not sure of, what I was not sure of, was whether the dislike of basketball had anything to do with its being played so much in the United States by blacks. Basketball was not my favorite game, so I had no real interest in opposing the ban. But I was thinking about people around me. The color issue came up in an insidious fashion, not with any in-your-face directness, more with a subtle and progressive recognition that the proscription of basketball just made no sense, and it was perhaps linked to a bias of which no one was particularly proud.

My reflection in these areas heated up somewhat when I heard the camp leadership's repeated insistence that we cut our bread before eating it. They served the traditional American white bread that was cut into the usual rectangular or square thin slices. They argued that it was a sign of good breeding when one cut that slice into halves or quarters before proceeding to eat it. I always wondered about the origin of that regulation, particularly in the context of an international camp, where campers were coming from different cultural backgrounds, and what was correct could never be so easily defined. Of course, I was right to be suspicious. My travels since then have long taught me that bread is eaten in many different ways all across the world.

The camp's leadership was still making an effort to do good and to promote harmony among us all. I appreciated that and noted one more time that religion was not a cornerstone of the endeavor. On Saturdays and Sundays, boys could attend a religious service of their preference in the nearby town, and some of us used the privilege. But within the camp activities themselves, the closest reference to a supreme being came at the beginning of the meals when we would sing a nonspecific chant thanking "you" for the meal. Some of the brightest and most cynical campers suggested to me privately that the chant had been developed by some of the camp leadership as a public testimonial to their beneficence. In other words, it was a patently self-serving song. I know my father would also have been suspicious, once they were so careful to steer around a reference to his God. My father always insisted that it was important to witness publicly about one's religious beliefs, since nonwitnessing could be tantamount to denial of one's Lord, a kind of subtle Saint Peter-like claim of ignorance while the cock was still crowing. With all of this said, I liked the camp experience. It introduced me to a wider world, one outside the Bajan precincts artificially set up in Brooklyn. And I was pleased the Sunday my father drove up to see me at camp. Young boys are always proud when their fathers testify publicly, even if silently, to their paternal commitment.

Boys High gave me one other wonderful opportunity when an adviser recommended that I present my candidacy for a debate forum run by one of the city's newspapers. Applicants came from all over the New York metropolitan area. I made the first cut, and we spent several weeks learning all about the formal way of running meetings, presenting ideas in a crisp oral fashion, and recognizing what motions took precedence over others as dictated by Robert's Rules of Order. We ultimately had to make oral presentations in order to win a spot in the final group. I felt good when I learned that I had made the grade. It was naturally from my father that I had borrowed the stylistic points I employed in my presentation. He should also take some pleasure in knowing that the top speaker was a young black man who went on to become a world-famous evangelist. This boy-preacher used his prodigious oratorical talent, which was already well developed then, for the glory of his God. I wonder how many boys, when faced with a new task or activity, enter it with the picture of their father in their minds, intent on imitating some aspect of what their father had done. In my case, I could always see my father in the act of talking, presenting orally, and using his hands to persuade his listeners of his rightness and his logic. This graphic image made it possible for me to face an audience.

The other important summer activity was the one-day excursion organized every year by Aunt Dais and some of her friends. I managed to attend only a couple of these events. I was away from Brooklyn much of the time in the summer months. The ones I did attend were of considerable social significance. They gave some Barbadians the chance to argue to themselves that the move to Brooklyn was worth it, after all. It was noticeable that the excursion brought a smile of relaxation also to Mamma's face.

The bus outing was usually organized to take place on a Saturday, and it was expected to leave early from Herkimer Street in front of Aunt Dais's house. But it could never leave on time, and for several reasons. First of all, some of the women came from faraway places like the Bronx, which meant they had to use the unpredictable weekend subway to get to Brooklyn. Secondly, that same morning, some of them were only finishing up the special cooking they did for the excursion. They couldn't leave home unless the peas and rice had come out the right way. Finally, personal preparations had to be taken care of: hair was being pressed at the last minute; the hem of a pair of pants needed to be shortened; or a blouse had to be matched to a skirt that was being borrowed from a girl-friend who hadn't turned up yet.

Men were in attendance at these excursions. But they never seemed to dominate the scenery like the women, who were decked out in the latest fashions, and ashimmer in gold bangles and chains. As the women themselves said, you had to look "stylish and purty, purty." It suggested that looking good meant the move to New York had been successful, on all possible levels. It required money to look the part and to buy the pro-visions for the excursion. A certain cheerfulness of spirit was also need-ed to get into the groove of a Bajan excursion, to offer one's own black pudding and souse for public consumption, or to present to the world one's special coconut bread or cassava pone to have the experts check it out. Then there were the women with their carefully prepared bottle of sorrel that they wouldn't offer to just anybody, or the other woman with the oxtails seasoned just right, brown in that heavy thick sauce I liked. It was obvious that the slightest sadness could throw one off-course and have a negative effect on the preparations.

Discussions started on the sidewalk even before the buses pulled off. Discussions in which Mary got introduced to a cousin of Martha, or Mary finally met the woman who bore John's child years ago, or Theodore introduced his new wife, who would be commented on with-out delay once the buses got moving and the appropriate noise could hide the opinions about this new wife. Some people, those who worked so hard throughout the year that they were rarely connected to the Bajan pipeline, might use the excursion to catch up on the latest news about Barbados.

"You see Theodore's new wife? I cyan believe he leff the woman who bring he childrun in dis world and raise dem sweet, sweet, sweet. An' den he went and marry dis ole woman wid she backside cock off."

"I agree wid you. He wife was a real nice, Christian, upstanding woman, and Theodore gone and leff she for dat?" (Followed by an exaggerated sibilant chupse.)

"But bosie-bo, dese men dis behave like real idiots sometimes. Yuh don't know where dese ideas does come from."

"Maybe dis new woman does do she ting real good. But dah en nuh reason to leff out de mudder of your own children. Dese men en got nuh conscience. And den deh does go and stand up in church and sing loud, loud, loud. Deh don know dat God can see dem?"

"But even if de woman know how to handle she business right, dat en nuh reason to leave de woman who bring children fuh he in dis world. Wuh he coulda keep de mudder of he children and do he ting on de side. He won't be the first man to do dat."

"I wonder if he providing for he children!"

This was an ethics-based analysis of Theodore's behavior, and he wasn't faring well. Of course, the final judgment was not surprising. Bajan women don't like to see one of their own so publicly scorned.

I never thought that the final destination of the buses was of much import, whether it was in Pennsylvania Dutch country or one of the parks in upstate New York. Bajans then didn't care where they went. They certainly needed good weather, so that everybody could dish out the food without being disturbed by raindrops falling into jug-jug or on top of plantains. But one could eat jug-jug anywhere. It was not important either that the destination be close to a beach. The women who dominated these events were not about to get their hair wet in anybody's foreign ocean. They didn't go to the sea much back home, so why would they go into the water elsewhere? Too much trouble to change clothes, take off all the jewelry, dry their skin afterward, get all the annoying sand out from everywhere that sand can get in, and also have to redo the hair that had been carefully coiffed at home.

"I look to you as though I en got nuh sense?" That was a common response of the women to the suggestion that they take a swim, as though it should be obvious why such a recommendation lacked common sense. With all this, Aunt Dais and her friends would pull off a wonderful event, and everybody would be content to have spent a long day being thoroughly Bajan, demonstrating that all the recipes were still well remembered, the rum still had its effect, and a "big-able" group of Bajans could have a wonderful time behaving like Bajans, like they back home, like they liming down in Bathsheba or up at the Crane.

The other event that Aunt Dais and her girlfriends staged was an annual calypso dance that was held in my time at the Gayheart Ballroom located just at the intersection of Nostrand Avenue and Eastern Parkway. Over the years, I attended other dances at venues in Manhattan and often in church halls in Brooklyn. But Aunt Dais's event was a special occasion that few Bajans could afford to miss, except those who lived too far away or those who were resolute nondancers like her own husband, Mr. Taitt. In those days, the men all wore suits, as though they were going to church. No sports jackets either. Serious suits. Dark suits, accompanied by a pair of comfortable shoes, because dancing was the focus of the night. The women were wrapped up in evening dresses, some long, some short, shoulders uncovered, and necklines plunging and showing more than I ever recall seeing at any other event in the winter.

Aunt Dais's dance wasn't like some cocktail sip where those attending had been specially invited by a hostess who had exercised a triage process to arrive at her guest list. This was a democratic affair, and I could tell that the Bajans present came from a multitude of different backgrounds. In the early evening, the music had the rhythm of the very early calypso art form, a sort of folksy, gentle beat that allowed partners to hold each other and pretend they were in the most elegant ballroom anywhere. That was when pastors like my own father would take to the floor, guiding their sedate wives or other female parishioners over the floor with ease and showing that they still had some life in the backbone.

"Reverend Griff, you like you tripping the light fantastic," would be gently uttered from the sideline by one of the pastor's parishioners.

My father replied, "Well the Rev still have a little life left in him, you know. Not enough to cut a rug, perhaps, but enough to show you that I remain blessed, young man."

And with that, my father steered his partner to another part of the floor.

The pre-World War II form of controlled calypso went on until the country crowd arrived. That's what I called them, the country crowd. I didn't really know what part of Barbados they hailed from, but I could tell that many of them had to be from the parishes far from Saint Michael. No city woman would accept an offer to dance, and before the man had gotten her on the floor, she'd be admonishing him.

"Don't mash my foot, hear, 'cause I got corns and dey hurting me real bad tonight."

"Wuh wrong wid you? I know how to dance. I en going nowhere near your corns."

Before the young man could hold her waist and indicate which step he was using, straight calypso or maybe a merengue-type step, she was already off to the races, as a buddy of mine used to say. So then the man had to adjust to whatever she was doing and catch up, because she was "wining" and not even looking at him. But it was evident the young fellow had learned that he had to take the women in hand, put down a strong "wine" himself, and gradually ease his partner into a groove, all the time having a look on his face that asked if she liked it and whether he was hitting the right spot, if you please. The answer came quickly enough when she smiled and consented to adjust her movement to his. But he had also encountered other women who stiffened the spine and backed off, each one making it clear she was on the dance floor with him but she was sure as hell "dancin' by sheself."

Everybody was soon perspiring. Certainly the sweat came from the obvious exercise. But I thought then that certain other elements contributed to the flow of perspiration everywhere. I always considered the oily fishcakes as a significant contributor, although I have no reason at all for this assertion. Then there was the hot sauce on drumsticks or on ham that helped. Finally, the Mount Gay rum fueled it all. Mamma always teased me because I never liked walking into these affairs holding the heavy, brown paper bags with grease marks all over them and the smell of fishcakes emanating from the bags. It seemed to contradict the business of putting on a suit. I did not understand how a man could put on a dressed-up suit and tie and then pick up a bag of fishcakes or patties. So Mamma enjoyed making the point that if I couldn't walk with the bags, then I shouldn't eat from them either, once the bags sort of found their way miraculously into the Gayheart. She also liked embellishing her argument with the claim that I likely learned the pretentious habit from my father, "walking with your long empty hands."

It is true that my father was not the type to walk into the Gayheart with a brown paper bag giving off the undeniable odor of fried food. Furthermore, no one would dare expect the Reverend to engage in that. What irritated Mamma, I'm sure, was that he never needed to take along anything in his hands to eat later on in the evening. If my father decided to go to any Bajan dance, he just needed to show up. All night long, women would be importuning him to taste one of their fishcakes. And every other male would invite him to join the fellas in a drink, a small one, of course, given his standing as a preacher, but with the look on their faces that suggested that if he drank with them, that very act would bless their little group and give them a little license to continue drinking. It was comical, but my father had standing in those days even at the Gayheart.

As the night wore on, the obligatory ceremony took place during which the members of the group who had produced the fête had to be introduced to all those present. I did not understand why it had to be organized with such seriousness of purpose. After all, youngsters like me had either connected to some female partner or still had hopes of doing so. In either case, a prolonged interruption of the music detracted from the objective of chatting with a lovely woman, regardless of the eventual outcome. Few of us wanted to acknowledge the reality concerning the potential outcome. For one thing, at these dances, one was much more likely to meet an older woman. And she, while having fun at the dance, was not about to embark on some serious business with a teenager. Then there was the high probability, too, of talking to a woman who lived far away from Brooklyn. That may have sounded romantic. But in practice it was highly inconvenient. Catching two subway trains to visit a woman wasn't amusing, either on one's way out to the house or on the return trip.

Nevertheless, this ritual of introducing the sponsors of the dance had to go on, and by interrupting the flow of the night, it irritated me. Each member of the organizing committee would half-dance up front to the beat of some made-up military march played by the band. The obligatory applause was given, as each member of the committee presented herself in a long gown, with a large identifying flower attached to the top of the dress. The brave among them might do a pirouette, anything to prolong the experience of being in the limelight. Some dignitary might say a few words, most of which could hardly be heard, because the audio system only worked well if everybody in a large hall like that would stay silent. That was an impossibility. Too much rum and fishcakes and hot sauce and sweating women and men who wanted to dance and "wuk-up." After all, the next day was church, and the day after that was work again or school. When was the next time one could hear Bajan music played by a live band?

Eventually, it had to happen. The band struck up "Las' Train to San Fernando," which might not even be the correct name of the piece, although it was always the line that people sang out. Everybody was on the floor, partner or not. It is then that you saw "wukkin-up." Or you felt it, because the floor was so crowded that you couldn't see very far. Then you could grab onto anything moving, old or young, church-going or not. Any port in a storm. There was storm everywhere, although given that we were on a dance floor in a public ballroom, the ports were all imaginary. But who cared? Arthritis gone, sent "through the eddoes," and people "wining" for spite. From the front or from the back, which you prefer? Church deacons hiding in the middle so you can't see them, and married women making moves under cover of the crowd that only their husbands ever saw before. That is what kaiso can do to you, as I know my father appreciated, even though the preacher in him would never let him affirm it publicly. My father was always sensitive about the business of public behavior. So I never saw him join the crowd in what we all used to call this "las' lap," this chance to dance the very last calypso for the night.

In the las' lap, the people on the edge of the dance floor, where they could be seen by the bystanders who were left, were upset. But that was their fault. You had to be ready, to anticipate when the las' lap was coming, so you could get a place of honor in the crowd, inside where the action was heavy, the movement steady and strong, and the perspiration flowing. What angers me now is to hear these young modern-day Bajans who think they invented the "wuk-up." What nonsense! And they come with their silly directions on the dance floor about "Hands in the air!" as though anybody really tuned into a calypso needs instructions about what to do. Furthermore, why would any sensible man dancing and grooving with a woman want to put his hands in the air? Even a preacher knows that, in that context, there must be a lot more interesting, more functional things to do with one's hands. But as usual, as my father and I have agreed from time to time, youth is wasted on the young. Say what you want, Aunt Dais and her lady friends used to throw one hell of a dance. As a Grenadian nurse once told me in the middle of the hospital in her capital city, "You ha to give Jack he jacket and Mary she bloomers." Aunt Dais knew how to throw a party.

But Aunt Dais did more than throw parties. On other occasions, she looked out for my interests. Aunt Dais sent me to her Bajan family doctor when I was sick, just as she had sent my father years before I arrived in Brooklyn. In giving me general advice, the doctor told me not to rush things because I might reach decisions too hastily. There was a lot to see before putting down anchor. He understood the pleasure of meeting people. However, he had no patience for romantic seriousness coming from adolescents.

He loved to regale me with stories about the long but productive road he had taken to becoming a physician. The first time I saw him as a patient he had no hesitancy in suggesting I wear a jacket when I came to his office. At first, I thought it was a joke. But he did not joke about such things. That's why he wore gray suits, in three-piece form all the time, with his watch chain hanging ceremoniously from his waistcoat, which Bajans pronounced "weskut." And when he went out, he put on his bowler hat. He was serious about the business of representation, much like my father. These Barbadian men of that generation, particularly once they moved away from the island of their birth, seemed to feel pressure to play a special role and represent values and symbolic styles that they thought were important. The doctor talked to me all the time and offered advice that was practical and earnest. His favorite story was about some other member of his class in medical school who dropped out in the final year because of love for a woman. My doctor couldn't understand how such a bizarre and serious act could be attributed to a love affair. In his scheme of things, first things were first. Love of a woman could never come before completion of studies and establishment of one's professional direction. Falling in love and not completing studies was madness, pure and simple. He also was persuaded that marriage after the completion of studies was often to a different type of woman, since the acquisition of a profession generally put one in a position to meet women of a higher status. I liked my talks with him, and I regretted not having him as a medical colleague after I had qualified. By then he was on his deathbed.

He was one of the voices that made it clear to me that I was expected to leave Boys High and go on to the university. My father did not ever oppose that direction. While I know he expected it, he never conspicuously sat down and helped me plan it. I suspect this was so, because the quarreling with Mamma had begun to distract him. I do not know how it started and who drew first blood. Sometimes they said more to each other than they should have, as husbands and wives do from time to time. It made no sense, and I could not understand it. In quarrels of this sort, the argumentation often lacks logic. Or even if it has logic, the opponents on both sides invoke arguments that are equally well articulated and buttressed. Much of the problem, to my mind, was in the move. Both of them longed for Barbados and were upset that they could not reproduce the island in New York, a metropolis that tore at every Bajan value they had once held dear.

CHAPTER EIGHT

The Portrait

In the fear of the Lord is strong confidence ...

Proverbs 14:26

There is on my desk at home a picture of my father that captures for me more facets of him than any other portrait. My father must have been about age forty when this black and white picture of him was taken. He was not alone. In it, he and his political colleague, Ernest Deighton Motley, were caught strolling confidently together outdoors, on their way, I believe, to Barbados's Government House, the official residence of the queen's representative in the island.

Their manner of dress meant that they were on official business. Mr. Motley wore a three-piece parson-gray wool suit set off by a dark tie with polka dots, and accented by a striking felt hat tipped ever so gently over his spectacles with the thick black frames that were his trademark. My father wore no hat, and his dark two-piece suit contained a vertical stripe that lightened the color of the fabric. The outfit was in turn brightened by a woolen tie with horizontal lines and a gold tie clasp. His jacket was buttoned and hugged his slim, tall frame.

The air is all business in the photograph. But its most telling characteristic is the confidence being exuded by the two men. My father knows he looks handsome, and he gives the impression that admirers are watching him from every angle. His movement is fluid, coordinated, and rhythmic, and muted power is suggested in the subtlety of the understated clothes. One might object that he is not wearing his clerical collar at the time. But the picture captures his determination to be somebody in the face of any obstacles. Since he is meeting with the governor of Barbados on that day, the resolute look on his face and the sense of purpose in his stride are understandable. He is seeing a representative of the queen, a political missionary from the upper stratum of Bajan society. My father is ready for him, as one would say then. Firm, confident, not apologetic for being there. He knows who he is and what his business is, and he is capable of measuring the man on the other side. As my preacher-sister recently told me about the photograph, "It translates an elegance of mind and a nobility of spirit," no doubt one of those ready-made expressions she had to be prepared to use on a moment's notice, like at some dinner when she is suddenly asked to bless the table.

The photograph is not of him and the governor. It is of him and a prominent politician of his time, a man who left his mark on Bajan politics and, I presume, on my father. I believe it was at least partly the interactions between the two of them that influenced my father's later decision to emigrate from Barbados to the United States. In the search to clarify who he was, my father recognized that it was in his interest to leave Barbados and its politics, to put distance between him and his own native soil, and some distance between him and Mr. Motley. The decision to leave, to implement his own self-imposed exile from an island he loved so much, was a distinctive part of elucidating who he was and ultimately claiming his own identity.

While in this picture, as I have said, my father was not wearing his pastor's collar, I know he took on the struggle of self-identification partly in religious terms. He sought clarity about himself by looking to his faith. It was a long time ago that he had his spiritual conversion. A close family friend who is now well into her eighties told me that when she first met my father and mother in Trinidad during the war, he was already a preacher. Another friend from the same generation confirmed that the Reverend was involved with Brother Tucker's church even before he left for Trinidad around 1943. So my father was baptized in the Spirit before I was born. His confidence then as a born-again

Christian must have begun to emerge when he was still a young man, although it obviously evolved as he grew older.

From several of the statements he made to me over the years, I concluded that in his view, his status derived partly from Biblical knowledge of who he was and what he had. He assessed himself as fortunate, because Jesus had got up on the cross and spilled His blood, something that meant a lot to my father. He had a way of classifying people based on how much the crucifixion business meant to them. He emphasized all that had been granted to him by God's grace and under the covenant of the blood, not the law.

Still, my father was so taken by the precepts and history of the Old Testament that I sometimes wondered why he hadn't converted to Judaism. Such a religious conversion would not have settled the other complex dimensions of his struggle to figure out who he was. Had he taken the step in religious terms, he would still have had to contend with what it meant to be a black Barbadian Jew; later in life he would have faced the problem of being a black Jew in the United States. So I understand that he stayed a devout Christian and mulled over to the very end of his life the idea that the Jews had a very special pact with God. This line of argument was always hard for me to digest, because it suggested that God inherently preferred one ethnic group to another. It may have been my simplistic and reductionistic understanding of my father's complex reasoning that led to my demand of fairness from God, that Jews and non-Jews have an equal shot at having a close connection to God. My father assured me that my demand was reasonable. He then ignored my concern about the special pact, leaving me to work it out on my own. I think he was quite content to have me mull over these complexities by myself, and in his self-satisfied, smug way to assure me that one of these days I would understand, when my faith had grown stronger and I was more in tune with the Spirit.

His struggle with the question of Jewish and Christian religious philosophy, at least in narrow application to his life, reminds me of James McBride's observations in *The Color of Water*, that wonderful text of biographical and autobiographical mixture. McBride's mother was a white Jew, who detailed her humiliation and degradation at the hands of a rabbi-father and later found her contact with Christianity as healing and liberating. Christianity lifted her up, forgave her, and made her new, teaching her that the God of her Christian black friends was the colorless color of water.

Yet, it was so obvious that this mother, as she delved more deeply into Christianity, recognized increasingly clearly that she could not efface her Jewish roots. Of course, she tried to rub out her origins. When her own family had had enough of her shenanigans with gentiles and blacks, the family sat shiva for her, cutting her off from them in all their Jewish righteousness. It must have pulverized her soul, especially since she knew so well what the ritual meant. But her contact with the black church helped her to visualize a God of oppression being transformed into an uplifting deity of mercy, redefining for a believer an identity that reflected full hope and promise. McBride's mother suggested some differentiation between Jewish and Christian God, a concept at which I imagine my father would have scoffed, since he liked to insist that oppression was always initiated by the self-centeredness of man and his stiff-necked rebelliousness against God's precepts. After all, my father understood well what the British had wrought throughout the colonial Caribbean. He saw all the sociopolitical and economic oppression as something carried out by men, white men, not by my father's just God.

His identification scheme was not simplistically and exclusively based on religion, since there were other dimensions to who he was. Over the years, the measuring of himself got sharper, more complicated, and I suppose more sophisticated. I comprehended that when I heard him say to someone, to a foreigner from Europe, and with the intent to be clarifying, that West Indians were a very unique group of black people. While he did not go on to articulate or delineate the characteristic features of each black subgroup with academic precision, he didn't have to. That look in his eye translated total confidence in his assertion about Barbadians. Over the years, I never had the slightest doubt that he knew what it meant to be a Barbadian. In the United States, he often used the term "West Indian" because it took too long to explain, to those who were commonly ignorant of Caribbean geography, where Barbados was located. People like myself who were close to him understood easily that while he may have said West Indian, he meant Barbadian.

Barbados was important to him, as were its cultural and political institutions. As a nonlawyer, he knew more about major cases before the

Barbados courts than anyone else in my circle. He was also aware of every overseas appointment in the Barbados diplomatic corps, and he followed all the major budget speeches given in the House of Assembly. He kept his finger on annual awards and honors; he knew the names of Barbados citizens knighted by the queen practically before the names were announced. And he maintained a steadfast commitment to conkies, coconut bread, and falernum with coconut water. I also doubt that it had ever entered his consciousness that rum was made anywhere else besides Barbados.

Racism was something he understood. He explained to me on many occasions how the economic classifications in Barbados were set up, how the economic distinctions often, although not always, conformed to color categories. From knowledge gained as a political associate of Ernest Motley in the 1940s and 1950s, my father told me about the moneyed whites who stood in the penumbra behind Mr. Motley, pulling strings that only the informed and experienced could see. So black and Bajan and Christian made for a combination that spelled considerable complexity for him. He appreciated that Barbados and the United States treated blacks differently. I eventually grasped at least one reason so many Barbadians and other West Indians who left their birth countries settled in the protective cocoon of New York's Brooklyn. They surrounded themselves with their familiar compatriots and culture, which made it easier to adapt to the struggles in the American workplace and to argue to themselves that while they were black, they were still West Indian.

We both noted on several occasions that listening to calypso music made us think about being from Barbados. We talked about the Bajan song called "Jack," a calypso to be more precise, in which the Mighty Gabby, one of my favorite practitioners of this distinctive West Indian art, tells his audience with delicious defiance that Barbadian beaches belong to local folk. Only the dispirited, blatantly ignorant, or blissfully arrogant ever thought it meant anything other than a clear warning to whites to stop carving up the beaches into territorial plots that belonged only to them. When Gabby, understandably mighty in his pulsating vernacular, asserted ownership over plain beaches, we knew he was staking out ground—geographic, intellectual, cultural, economic, and political territory. Gabby was signifying, identifying himself, to the resounding appreciation of every black Bajan on the island, except those of course who had an interest in having the beaches be off-limits to black people. "Da beach is mine, mine, and only mine," Gabby intoned. He addressed himself directly to Jack, a nom de plume for the symbolic embodiment of attempted power and control over plain Bajans, particularly those feeling disenfranchised and without influence: "… the beach belong to we." And to buttress his claim, Gabby made it clear, that in contradistinction to non-Bajans, his navel string was interred on Barbados. If that was hard for some listeners to assimilate, then there was the more traditional way to make the argument. His father and mother used to bathe at that beach, which was to argue methodically that the privilege of bathing there was divinely passed on to him. That's talking about authenticity, about personal definition and ownership, about laying claim to what our forebears left us.

My father had a strong feeling about that argument, not only with respect to the political dimensions, but particularly with regard to this special affinity Bajans have for areas of their coral rock. So when that other calypso talks about Bush Hall and Bank Hall and Eagle Hall and Shot Hall, it's a recitation of names that represent places known only to the informed Bajan and that speak of personal connections to the island home. I have never forgotten how my father used to enjoy reciting the names of all the sugar factories located on the island and placing them specifically in the parish where they were geographically located. As the years went by, the economy changed, and many of the factories closed down, he would take a certain delight in identifying the precise name of a factory that used to be, with accompanying data that would interest only the historian, but which set him off as the informed insider. He liked, too, to let me know when he had acquired knowledge about the factory, because he had been there with the Boss. He would take on the facial look that suggested he knew how the engines worked and that he had personally met the man who managed the factory long before I was born. He was proud of this private knowledge that connected him to the Boss.

There are elements that facilitate maturing of West Indian identity, such as the connection to antecedents like mother and adult neighbors. Other factors can weaken one's identity and ultimately cause its deterioration, such as the relentless humiliation by colonial arrogance, or the intolerant prejudice, sprung from ignorance, of former friends and neighbors. I am pleased that my father did not show signs of any identity disintegration. When my father recognized that he was dying, he talked about wanting to be buried back home where he'd grown up. Actually, all he said was "home." We all knew it meant where he had grown up. We also knew the grave site would be where the Boss was already interred.

Some people won't ever forgive him for wanting to die back home, in Barbados, not New York where he had earned his bread for about forty years. Although he had carried a U.S. passport for a long time, he decided that on the very inside of himself, he was just not American. In my own mind, I find nothing wrong with that. He certainly took from the Americans. But he also gave to them and to the broader society. As the saying goes, he was a productive member of society, and he worked hard.

In 1997, I was in Barbados at the time that the visiting English were humiliating the West Indies test cricket team. I went to a jewelry store trying to find a duty-free watch for a friend who had done a kindness for me. I struck up a conversation with several strangers in the boutique, very easy to do when the whole island was bedazzled by a West Indies team at wit's end, lacking purpose and direction, simply doing everything wrong, and being thrashed by the unrelenting skill of their former masters. Strangers were beseeching my help, wanting to know what balm could restore their pride. That was a day when usually sedate ladies were uttering to just anybody within hearing that they didn't know what "de rasshole da West Indies team was doing." They also suggested that "a lash in dey ass" might right things, which was at least more hopeful than some of the men who dared utter the unthinkable: Take on some other nationality, be anything but a West Indian being taught a lesson in cricket so harshly and so publicly, having one's slightly ballooned self so conspicuously deflated. If my father had been alive, he would have mocked what he called those fair-weather supporters. For him, a cornerstone of true identification was its constancy. One had to live and die with one's team and country.

I like Robert Stepto's use of the term "personal geography" to label this process of plunging into the task of identifying self. His term conveys a sense of uncovering and the importance of place, of palpating the physical terrain while contemplating the nonpalpable aspects of the environment. The term also suggests the impact of one's being in different places at different times. I'm fascinated by what one does with the meaning derived from self-identification. We certainly have many recent examples of how the clarification of identity and the differentiation of self from others can lead to destructive impulses to protect self and one's group while killing others. The celebrated black American psychoanalyst, Charles Pinderhughes, recognized that tendency early and warned of its being employed in the service of paranoia and prejudice. Frantz Fanon and others also saw the clarification of self as a fundamental first step in avoiding slavery and its milder imitations. Besides all that, the Caribbean islands are clearly in an increasing uproar. It makes sense that, given the unique history of this region, people want to take stock of where they are and who they are, so that some reasoned conclusion can be made about where to go next. That's obviously a part of the crucial point: Knowing who you are helps clarify what you want to do about your tomorrow self, about your children, about the broader society, about what the French so blithely call the "descendance" and the "patrimoine." My father agreed that the elaboration of identity wasn't just about figuring out whether he was black or white.

Two recent cultural events in the Caribbean highlight this work of identifying self and then visualizing its application in practical terms. The first event has been at the eye of the debate in Barbados (similar arguments are readily found elsewhere in the Diaspora) about what to do with the statue of Lord Nelson that has been a constant geographic fixture in Bridgetown of my boyhood.

"Man, John, we should get rid of that ridiculous statue. It don't have much to do wid we history. And he does stand up deh looking like he is lord of all dat he surveys. Including lord o' we. Dat en right. Not in de 21st century. Dat statue got to go."

"Brenda, dat is not a fair argument. Regardless of what Nelson do, we come along and see he here. He part of we history. We grow up wid he. We cyan just ignore he like dat. You cyan be so intellectually dishonest. He part of we culture."

"Say what you like, John. I en want nuh white man in de center o' town like dat. Why you cyan be proud and put statues of black people up deh so we childrun kin grow up feeling proud o' deh black fore-bears?"

"Brenda, you sidestepping the argument. Nelson history is we own. And once you start putting up black people statues, you gon only start a riot 'bout here. De political parties in dis island cyan agree 'bout which black people deserve honors. You mekkin' sport. Tearing down a white man statue is easy. But putting up a black man statue is something else all together."

My father held the opinion that Barbados did not pay enough respect to local Bajans of both genders who had opened up pathways originally controlled by the British. He always knew who the first Bajan chief justice was, the first matron at the hospital, and so on. Those were his heroes.

The second event relates to the question of whether Caribbean countries should develop their own form of final appellate court so as to avoid any further need to seek judicial guidance from Britain's Privy Council, an institution that bitterly reminds some about the old days when London held sway with divinely inspired confidence. Complaints about the lethargic round-trip movement of appeals between the Caribbean and London can be couched in judicial prose. Nevertheless, the linkage of identity to the resultant solution is self-evident. How could the Privy Council not be seen as a colonialist structure having impact on the lives of Afro-Caribbeans? While my father's connection to Barbados was clear and definite, he kept a solid share of ambivalence for Britain. Certainly he loved so many of its rituals, so much of its culture. But he disliked with predictable intensity the idea that the British, and not Barbadians, should perform certain tasks. When the task was sociopolitical or intellectual, my father felt it was an offense against God to claim that the British could do it and Barbadians could not. Resorting to the British Privy Council was destructive to the solid devel-opment of Barbadian identity.

My father also talked from time to time about the notion of island character. His occasional comments remind me of an instructive chat I had recently with a Trinidadian colleague. After a few pleasantries, I turned the conversation to a calypso I knew was fairly old. Snippets of it were running through my head, but I couldn't get the lyrics straight. Neither could I recall exactly who had sung it, although I thought it had been born in Trinidad. It had to do with meat and rice, and I was captivated by the memory of it because I knew it was connected to identity. So I prodded and got what my colleague could conjure up about the song.

As my colleague had it, a Trini and a Bajan were doing a cook-up, with the local chap providing the rice and the Bajan offering up the meat. Ignoramus as I am in matters of this sort, I was reminded that meat imparts flavor to rice, and one doesn't opt to cook plain rice if it can be avoided. In addition to the complex of taste and odor that spiced-up meat provides, everyone knows in a plain ordinary way that the sum of meat and rice surpasses rice alone. So I was pleased by the notion that a Bajan's national character would have him showing so much generosity of spirit that he would give meat to the communal cause in order that everybody might benefit.

My colleague's version of the song had the two men eventually getting into an argument. It culminated in the Bajan's demand that his meat be returned, which on the face of it translates a clear vexatiousness of spirit. In Bajan parlance, then, "the man get vexed—vexed fuh so," to the point that "he tek up he meat and he gone. The cook-up brek up." But in addition to the obvious treachery of taking back his meat, it should be obvious—and we know it in the Caribbean—that you can't take a piece of meat cleanly out of a pot of rice. Grains of rice stick to the meat; so in the act of pulling out his cut of meat, the Bajan was essentially getting back more than he put in. Hence the loan or sharing of the meat was transformed into an act of spite and malice.

This took my colleague and me into ruminations about island character. I was told plainly that a Bajan was seen as mean-spirited, and a Jamaican will start a fight over nothing. The Trinidadian was said to be tricky, although I wasn't sure whether this included both the East Indian and Afro-Trinidadian sides. My colleague said little about the other islands, although I had an experience recently in Barbados that related to one of the other islands. Several women were just relaxing while one of them regaled the others with stories about her mistreatment of her current boyfriend. I nonchalantly asked one of the women what she would do if in that context of humiliation, the man retaliated physically. Without the slightest pause, she asked me whether I thought she was a Guyanese, which is to say one born and brought up in Guyana. I had to ask for clarification, although by the set of her face and the glaring haughtiness in her eyes, it was clear to me that she was not about to accept a beating from any man. I have no idea about the origin of the term "Guyanese" in this situation. But there it is, another expression about national character, whether true or false. Now the humor in the calypso I was describing earlier is there. But it doesn't entirely efface the puzzling heaviness of being at least partly defined at a national level by elements out of one's control.

Teachers also had an impact on the development of identity in old-time Barbados. I recall how my teacher at Saint Giles would assign a poem for the class to memorize at home. Next day he'd call on us, skipping from one boy to the next, oblivious to the fact that some boys were terrified of public performance, and others were paralyzed by the anticipatory anxiety, the certain knowledge of what had transpired the last time they forgot a line of a poem. In my class, when a student forgot a part of the poem, he went to the middle of the classroom and awaited the end of the exercise. By then, there was a line of boys all knowing what was coming, trying to decide whether they wanted their six lashes on palms of hands or on their backs. The leather strap, harsh and unforgiving, would fall, less heavily than a ton of bricks, but with no feathery lightness either. It wasn't crushing, more like a cross between a sharp bite and a quick cut. And the teacher supposedly cared! I didn't believe it then, despite my father's assurances. I bristled too at the suggestion that on growing older, I would come to appreciate the beating. My father loved to say that to me, although I wonder now if he was talking more to the Boss, who I understand liked something about the act of flogging.

While I was a little preoccupied by my teachers' violence, I was more centered on their general harshness. They never laughed, those teachers; they never patted my head affectionately. I recall they did smile in unnecessarily solicitous exchanges with the few women who taught the very young boys. Yes, they told me I was bright. That was one thing in Barbados. They would always tell you when you were bright, even if they told you so with the chilliness of the wind blowing across Bathsheba beach in Barbados at five o'clock in the morning. But they also had a way of telling the others that they weren't very bright, that they had a hard head. I wondered why so many teachers saw the world through such an unjoyful lens. And I was concerned that the poorest and the blackest boys got the severest beatings.

My teachers at Saint Giles Boys' School were not a group of tyrants. In fact, they prepared us well for the transition to secondary school. It's just that they had so little time for the boys who didn't catch on fast. The teachers could have given more consideration to the idea that the boys who were not bright still had the task of growing into men. In this system, the intelligent, good-looking, coordinated boy seemed to get all the breaks. The chubby, not so good-looking, clumsy lad often had a troublesome row to hoe, and teachers could be unsupportive in their dealings with these children. The other community socializing agents played their roles too. Adults would hone in on defects, physical or other, with a precision that made us children blanch.

"Boy, you know you have a big head. You en growing nuh more?"

Observations, and public ones at that, were made about bandy legs, thin hips, and flat backsides. The list could be exhaustive in a village with really sharp tongues. We youngsters absorbed the vocabulary with an amazing quickness, because we felt we had to know the words to defend ourselves against anticipated onslaughts. Regularly the best defense was an unrelenting attack. I felt sorry the day those young boys picked on one of their own, because his backside was large, and he strutted with it "cock off," as we used to say, meaning it stuck out too much. So they asked him if he was a buller, as though any of them had the slightest idea what homosexuals did together. Of course, the intent was to hurt. But if the village was in my time the reservoir of so much that detracted from the facile development of personal identity, I wonder what it must have been like in my father's time.

I return to the school context in Barbados only to make the point that in many conversations, my father and I praised the technical educational objectives of Bajan schools. Bright boys did learn things where I went to school, and they became significant contributors throughout the world. I am less confident about how to characterize the modest achievers and how to epitomize the struggles of the disadvantaged to find their place and themselves amid so many signals that they belonged to no one and no place of consequence. My father's generation was justifiably preoccupied with the difference between local black Barbadians on the one hand and British whites and their local descendants on the other. I became sensitized to the distinctions between the Bajan upper and middle classes and everybody else.

I recognize that Barbadian life has changed in the past fifty years. Television, radio, travel, computers, tourism—all these elements have had an impact on the youth of the island. They are no longer unambiguously hostage to the narrowly focused information spun by the formal and informal cadre of Britons exported to the Caribbean every year. The British cleverly transmitted their values through a number of institutions and rituals. For example, I couldn't escape the influence of the cadet corps at school even though I never joined the group. The ramrod-straight backs of the cadets and the obvious military discipline inherent in the slow march were all British. I felt it around the cadets. I saw it the day my father took me with him to visit his high-ranking policeman friend. We got to the house early. Then the car drove up, and the captain got out. The driver, a mere police constable, also got out without dallying and exchanged words quickly with the captain, then froze at attention, bringing up his legs and seeming to ram his feet one after the other into the pavement. Then he saluted. What amazingly British behavior, I thought.

With these images in mind, I could understand why my father and so many old-time West Indians had trouble with the dreads, when these adherents of Rastafari made their appearance on the Barbadian social scene. Dreadlocks were un-British. They wouldn't suit the cadets or even the scouts. And to imagine dreadlocked choirboys walking up the aisle in any Cathedral choir? The imagery is discordant, disjunctive—ultimately threatening to someone like my father, and of course, it is intermingled with race matters. Now that is an ancient view of dreads, one that has been considerably refashioned by recent generations of West Indians. But even in that time, dreads would not have been worn in a Broad Street bank, probably not even by those keeping the place clean and tidy. This attitude of the establishment, of those in charge, would not have upset my father, who had strong feelings about one's appearance and sense of orderliness, which in his mind were always linked to British traditions. My father was at ease with his captain of police and all the regimented behavior.

My mother's view of all this is worth some consideration. She never thought much of what she saw as the long, unkempt plaits of dreadlocked Barbadians. She had heard about the back-to-Africa movement. However, she had not seen Africa and did not wish to go there. She was acutely aware of being black, of being dark-skinned, and she talked about it often. On the other hand, talk about the black Diaspora felt vaguely ludicrous to her. She had spent some of the war years in Trinidad, coping with a culture there that often felt palpably foreign to her, on an island literally next door to Barbados. So what was this about brotherhood across the wide oceans, based on some theoretical harnessing of common feelings and similar experiences? She had enough to do in following God's agenda in her local vineyard. Globalization was a concept invented to distract her from hard work and a Christian commitment to her family and village neighbors.

A friend of my father once asked him to put up a visitor as a kindness. My father obliged, naturally, and my mother made space for the woman in the girls' bedroom. But eventually the guest, who was from another Caribbean island that nobody in our family had ever seen, started carrying out practices that showed, at least to my mother's satisfaction, an adherence to peculiar religious beliefs. In my mother's mind, her children were possibly at some risk from this foreigner. So with a certain predictability, a quarrel eventually broke out, with my mother raising her voice and making threats in a way I'd never seen before. The woman had to leave, guest or not. Furthermore, it was clear to my mother that the woman was no neighbor. My mother felt no connection to the woman's strange beliefs. There was no agreement about identity between the woman and my mother.

My parents repeatedly made it clear that their children had to look as though they had a mother and a father. This was their way of talking about identity and self-esteem. For them, it had nothing to do with finances, or at least only minimally so. Of course, one needed money to buy clothes, which in their scheme of things, with their God looking on, was eventually taken care of. The principal task was to safeguard what the good Lord had blessed them with, which caused them to devise clever techniques. For example, I had home clothes, school clothes, and Sunday clothes. I could eat ackees, cashews, or mangoes while I was dressed in home clothes. When I was wearing my Sunday clothes, I could not get involved with fruit that stained or temporarily discolored clothing. That was an act of aggression in my parents' eyes, a declaration of war against their household rules, a suggestion of infantile madness. As they said, with a glorious sense of confident mockery: "You can run now, but you still have to sleep home." That was their way of telling me that I would pay the price for such folly. Sunday clothes were sacred. Everybody knew it. A child's clothes had to last long, unsullied, washed and ironed by Miss Garner's old iron, the one heated on a coalpot. This rule was observed throughout every neighborhood I knew, which cannot possibly be true, except I couldn't imagine any young boy eating a staining fruit in any Sunday white shirt he had. Doing so in school clothes could happen at school or on the way to school, but not at home. My parents' rules were therefore sharply lucid and explicit, and their sense of simple elegance transcended financial constraints. Their view was elementary and definitive: "Because yuh poor, yuh don have to look like yuh en got nuh family."

My father expanded on that with a smoothness that reflected what he did in his own life and how he thought about self-identification. He talked to me several times about wearing whatever one had with style and flair. He didn't mean flamboyance. I figured out fairly quickly that he always kept his eye on the leaders of the community. One should look like a part of the upper crust without having their money. This wasn't just about clothes. It was about overall deportment, which is why my father read so voraciously and cultivated ways of carrying head and waving hands that reflected confidence. He often told me that people always treated with the utmost deference those who looked comfortable in their skin and sure of belonging in places of esteemed status. He made it practically a point of honor to go places neatly dressed, looking handsome, but without a farthing in his pocket.

Concerning experiences that detract from the development of self-esteem and clarity, it is striking that in my early years, I experienced no structured impediments to entering major societal institutions in Barbados. From Saint Giles Elementary School I went on to Harrison College and rubbed shoulders confidently with the students who were there. It could have been Trinidad's Queens Royal College or Britain's Eton. It would have made little difference on the academic side of things. There was also no hesitancy about going to church, and no difficulty shopping at Cave Shepherd or Harrison's, although most people I knew would have first checked the cheaper prices of the Swan Street stores or seen what Mr. Layne at the Civic Cooperative Society had to offer. These acts of freedom were essential to my father's view of life. He thought that freedom of access to the major institutions in the society was a principle that defined the greatness of the tiny island of Barbados.

This did not mean to my father or to me that there were not some other unwritten rules or mechanics that influenced how things happened. I joined the Barbados Sea Scouts, because my eldest brother had been a member. I might have joined the Harrison College Scout Troop or the one at the YMCA. But I knew I would never have tried to join the Garrison Troop, where white boys did their thing. I use "white" loosely, because I long ago learned that in the Caribbean, skin shading can be complicated by hair type and shape of one's nose. If posed the question—Did the Garrison Scouts ever reject me or tell me I could not join them?—I would have to reply honestly that I simply never applied. This was no different from my observation, since I was a football fanatic, that Carlton and Pickwick clubs had no black players. So when a white Harrison College teacher, newly arrived from England, announced he was a football enthusiast and made it clear on game days that he could handle several of us youngsters without giving up the ball, I knew he wasn't going to play for Empire or Spartan, the premier black clubs.

The clearest unwritten rule applied to the beaches at the Aquatic Club and the Royal Yacht Club, places where no blacks I ever knew set foot. When strong swimmers like me swam out to the farthest point on the jetty of the Aquatic Club and climbed up on it so we could squeal in delight and jump off, a black watchman eventually appeared and ordered us to stop. We then retreated, confused and disoriented by the experience. I never even took it up with my father and complained that I wasn't allowed to utilize the beaches of those two select clubs. Mamma would have resorted to her usual conservative homespun logic and would have asked me why, with all the beautiful beaches in Barbados, I needed to go play on a little stringy piece of white sand that a few white people needed to feel they controlled? Of course, beachfront property in Barbados now costs a small fortune, which would never have meant very much to her mind. Put all that aside, the non-entrance to the Aquatic Club's beach taught me a lot about difference.

My father believed that all Barbados was open to him. He used to enjoy surprising us a bit on bank holidays when he was taking us all around the island in his small Austin motorcar. He would turn into the most unexpected driveways, the long ones in the country usually shrouded by tall fruit trees and eventually ending at a lovely plantation house. I would stay shyly in the car, because I never ceased to associate these long driveways with big Alsatian dogs. But my father would park and get out, unafraid, confident. The owner of the house would quickly show up and effusively welcome the Reverend and offer drinks and cookies of some sort. My father had a sense of what was proper. So he always left after about a half hour, while his host still had something interesting to say. My father knew he had shown up without an invitation and he did not wish to overstay his welcome, as he said. He also had no intention of behaving in a way that suggested he was contemptuously familiar. The owner of the plantation house was not a friend. The individual was someone my father knew, but not a close friend, not a buddy. Still, my father understood how to teach the lesson that all Barbados was open and accessible, while still emphasizing the puzzling contradiction that there was a difference between groups.

He and Ernest Motley are so proud in the picture, relaxed in their English wool suits. Neither one of them is perspiring or showing any signs of fatigue. They look like two diplomats on a mission.

The Aquatic Club experience, and others over the years, had hurt, but without destroying the remarkable reality that I remained deeply Bajan, connected to the coral rock and to my father in a way that is hard to explain to others. There is also no denial that I have long made a life, an adult life, outside of Barbados. But the outside life and the inside life are not the same.

CHAPTER NINE

Holding Strain

The Lord is my light and my salvation; whom shall I fear? The Lord is the strength of my life; of whom shall I be afraid?

Psalm 27:1

There are customs that were always important to my father and me that have been eroded in Barbados with the passage of time. Alterations in these traditions also say something about change in the broader culture. I harbor a certain resentment, because the change means that a piece of us has gone by the board, which makes me want to ask rather irritably who recommended the change and who was persuaded that the change really constituted improvement. Of course, both my father and I recognized that there are numerous forces constantly at work on the cultural scene of any country. Furthermore, not all the forces are local in origin and thus presumably subject to the influence or control of personalities and institutions we know. A technological development that originates halfway round the world can now have solid impact in Barbados. All this is to say that adhering to the old order is no easy matter, even if we could all be in agreement about what we wanted to keep. But I have my own idea of cultural practices that deserved to be maintained, customs that put my father and me together in a way I liked, very different from the Sunday morning cleaning of the places where chickens put down their eggs or where pigs left their waste.

However, that is precisely the point. Maintaining the symbols of a relationship between father and son can't be done without reinforcing of the rituals and cultural practices that justified the very existence of the symbols. This requires that certain things we used to do together remain feasible. And if they are not doable, because he is no longer here, then they should still remain possible in my memory's view, at least. I like the idea of holding on to memories and going through the repetitive motions in my head that make the memories come to life and become palpable, even as everything else deteriorates. I like holding on, or as Bajans often say, holding strain, keeping the thought going, sustaining the action that fuels the memory. It is an addiction. And I concede it.

For example, Barbados no longer celebrates that special Guy Fawkes Day on November 5, when Mamma and every other mother up in Station Hill used to make conkies, and the children would play with anything that sparkled or made noise and vaguely resembled fireworks. The connection of that celebration to its origin in England and some attempt to blow up the British Parliament got more and more tenuous with every passing year. But that was never the point for my father and me. What I liked was the way it brought together our family, centered us on a marvelous ritual of eating a specific dish prepared by a loving mother, and magnified my father in the children's eyes as a caring father who came home with the fireworks that amused us for a very fleeting period of time. He would pull up in the old Austin motorcar, park it, and get out, his arms full of little paper bags. They were transparent enough for us to identify the ones holding the little bombs. Others were not deep enough to hide the "starlights"—those thin sticks, attached to which was the material we would light with a match, causing a burst of shimmering light to explode. It was a child's dream of bringing stars once a year under control in Station Hill.

Every child has these bittersweet occasions when he mounts a prodigious struggle against time and tries to preserve the pleasure of the moment, one provided by a present father. I have referenced it before as I confronted bakes and a tempting fried egg. On Guy Fawkes Day, I used to put the four or five bombs in my pocket that were mine, all mine, and then I tried to enjoy the explosions provided by the bombs of others before using up my own limited stock. It was my childish way of holding on dearly to what I had, to his gift. It was not an act of selfishness in that I did not wish to share with others. It was more an act of desperation to prolong the pleasure of the special occasion. The time would come, it always came, when I had to give in and use what I had. Then I would remove from my pants pocket the small bomb the size of a big marble, caress it gently, then wind up and crash it against the wall. The explosive sound would come, as would my breath of satisfaction at a well-placed throw, because sometimes hesitancy in the throw would make the bomb glance off the wall and not explode, unleashing a flurry of activity to find the unexpended bomb in our semi-dark yard. Once exploded, there was nothing left except the residue of smoke, tinged with the smell of gunpowder. Then nothing. Nothing at all.

This forced me to delve into the remainder of my small stock that was being progressively depleted. It was unadulterated cruelty, but still God's way of teaching me that it was in the order of things that nothing lasts forever, including a father's presence. This rule applied to all pleasure, and especially straightforwardly innocent enjoyment like that. But others got the last laugh, because they took away that fireworks night. They replaced it with what? Nothing that brings families together in places like Station Hill, with young children running all over the place, and mothers offering conkies, and fathers showing up with a meager gift. The fireworks were not grandiose, not expensive, not elaborate. But he always brought them. Guy Fawkes should have been forgiven his act of treachery. At least, children like me thought so.

The use of cornmeal to make conkies was an important and sacred ritual in our home. Every house in Barbados had its own version of a conkie. Little boys like me, who in that generation never objected to being kept out of the kitchen, did not learn what proportions guided the mixing of the cornmeal with nutmeg, essence, pumpkin, and other ingredients. Some cooks prepared them in banana leaves; others used that special kind of wax paper that existed then. Some people put raisins in their conkies; for others, plainness was a sign of almost religious purity. My father agreed with me and buttressed my simplistic belief that nobody made a conkie like Mamma. I have no doubt that every Bajan will laugh at that assertion. So let them laugh. Not even the fancy cooks at Government House could make a conkie like Mamma's. That is my parochial view of things. And there it stands. As a matter of fact, I am confident that the only body—the Station Hill way of saying the only person—who would put the conkies made by other people above the conkies made by his mother is a body who wasn't raised in a serious family. My father appreciated the notion that no erudite conkie eater, no sophisticated consumer of Bajan conkies, no one who had ever witnessed the profound act of making conkies, would glibly accept conkies from outside as superior to the homemade version. Conkies evoked a certain loyalty to the home base. Even though I have eaten many of them, describing the consistency and the taste of a conkie to a non-Bajan remains a puzzling task, the equivalent of trying to explain to a nonbeliever what it is like to be touched by the Holy Spirit. The more one tries, the more tongue-tied one becomes. A conkie tastes like a conkie.

Despite the powerful effect that the connection of fireworks and conkies has had on my memories of father and childhood, there is a certain logic to the expectation that Guy Fawkes Day would eventually be dropped, as Barbados became independent and sought to construct her own holiday celebrations. But in doing so, a part of my father and me got consumed in the process.

The newfangled holidays don't make any sense to me now. They don't magically conjure up memories that bring my father and me together in that old-time way. The annual July Crop-Over Festival may bring together twenty-five thousand people to witness the crowning of the Calypso Monarch, a cultural success by any measure. But it means little to me because I cannot share it with him or Mamma. I expect that in time, another generation will speak with hushed reverence about Crop-Over.

The other example to which I cling tenaciously is the celebration of the Agricultural Exhibition that used to go on in Queen's Park in December. It was a special moment for us. My father would give me a few dollars, meaning two or three, and I would walk up and down for hours looking at the girls, chatting with my buddies, playing the games of chance, and trying to look cool. In that day and age, being cool was a simpler task than now. One year, for example, nylon shirts were the rage, so many boys in that park were wearing a nylon shirt. I sported a white one, made from material that Mamma had bought at the Civic store in Swan Street. Elwin and Junior had shirts of different colors and finer material, as befitted their status of being older. Anyhow, Queen's Park was ablaze in color, as all these older and younger boys were showing off their new shirts with an accompanying carriage that suggested they thought they looked good in the eyes of onlookers. We boys were "styling," a Bajan expression translating as contentment and pride through a form of village fashion.

In those days, of course, no young boy I knew resorted to being cool through violence. That was not even a conceptual possibility. It is true that male muscles were displayed by some I knew who used to lift weights, and who tried to imitate pictures of men seen in magazines advertising Charles Atlas exercises. But those muscles could not be used to intimidate anybody. The essence of cool in my day was manifest in the unique gait that we displayed on occasions such as the Exhibition. The walk was additionally enhanced by a few limited options at our disposal. Some boys liked first to turn up the collar of the shirt, then dip one shoulder down, while the other stayed in place. Other boys raised both shoulders and curved them forward so that their back took on a somewhat rounded appearance. There was, too, the choice of one hand, both hands, and no hand in the pants pockets. Occasionally, a daring youngster would drape a scarf ever so elegantly around his neck or tie it around his waist. The strut would then come. One boy I knew had perfected the art of dragging one leg slightly behind the other, which never failed to attract the gaze of passing girls. I had to give him credit for engaging in the complex coordination of different groups of muscles being used at the same time. While dragging one leg slightly behind, he moved an arm in a way that seemed to inscribe a semicircle in space, while dipping the contralateral knee. He must have seen a medical movie showing some family suffering from a neurological disease characterized primarily by what the experts call a movement disorder. It was not something I would ever have tried, since up in Station Hill, mothers would call that mocking God and would suggest that God just might leave you walking that way permanently. So I left that sort of "styling"— as we used to call it—alone.

I was never interested in the agricultural dimension of the Exhibition. It did not make any sense to me, was not important, that a particular farm or plantation might be proud of what it was growing or producing up in the country. I could not describe the difference between eddoes and yams or between circee bush and green-tea bush. I was more taken by the all-encompassing task of getting to meet some girl whom I admired and wanted to engage in conversation. I heard stories told in hushed tones by the older boys about escorting their girlfriends out on the dark pasture away from monitoring eyes. Apparently things would go on that would put conspiratorial smiles on the boys' faces. But I never knew whether the stories were entirely true, partly true, or blatantly false. I will say that as the years went by and I gained my own experience, the stories made those older boys look like better performers than would be expected under such trying circumstances. In retrospect, the boys had to have been puffing up their resumés a bit. Besides, I never heard from the girls, who in those days would never have dared to give voice (certainly not to a boy) to their participation in such exploits. There was obviously no way of obtaining an objective assessment, or at least a view from another angle, of the activity that reportedly turned mere boys into sophisticated Don Juanesque characters.

Having said all that, how could the authorities have done away with my Exhibition? My father played a prominent role in making the Exhibition a central celebration for me. Once, I arrived there at the entrance to the Park, and the line was long and moving very slowly. It seemed as though they weren't letting anybody in. My father showed up, and the keeper of the gate immediately recognized him and cracked the gate slightly so he and I could pass, unfairly ahead of the waiting line, of course. This was our private fête, something the authorities could never have really understood. In fact, it is one of the remarkable dimensions of these experiences. Adults put together an event or celebration of some sort. However, they have no well-formed idea of how youngsters take the event and refashion it to their own liking. Oh, adults knew we liked the Exhibition, but they didn't know deep down how much we looked forward to it, how much it entered our daydreaming lives. Adults would have forgotten how we practiced our walk, the carriage, the slope of the shoulders, and the sag of the hips that would in our hopes bring smiles to the lips of our admirers.

My father comes to mind frequently when I think about changes in Barbados institutions such as churches and schools. Sunday, which long ago was the exclusive prerogative of the church, is now being fought over with a vengeance. Most observers seem in agreement that the church is losing the battle, if not the entire war. This is a tension that my father talked about often. He still believed in the idea that Sunday was the Lord's Day, and only certain specified activities could legitimately be carried out on that day. That's why I never played cricket or soccer on Sundays, and paying visits to my grandfather was a defined Sunday ritual. My father reasoned that once these Sunday activities were expanded to include others, there would eventually be a deterioration in the values the society held dear.

Authorities in many countries are now arguing about how to keep children with weapons out of the schools. My Bajan compatriots who have spent years as educators are troubled by the idea that schools are no longer oases in a troubled secular society. Schools are becoming part of the battleground, and their protective capacity is being eroded. This makes me long for the school and the religious edifice of yesteryear, a thought that would make my father laugh were he to hear me say this. He would no doubt characterize it as a grudging concession to the church, even if not the school.

There is something so comforting about the Barbadian institutions of fifty years ago. For years, I went off to Harrison College in the morning much earlier than was necessary. I went to play kneeling-down cricket or marble cricket with my friends. There again, it was marvelous how we took an adult game and made it into our own. The bat was probably a third of the usual size, obviously necessitated by the fact that the batter was kneeling down. I never even asked who made those cut-down bats, although I assumed that some boy had a relative who was good at carpentry. The ball was a small hopping-ball. Or it was one made of tar or some other substance and then covered with a sort of padded exterior that made it soft on impact.

On certain occasions, the time afforded me by such an early arrival at school was used to complete homework, more often than not to work out mathematics problems that would not be figured out by the creativity of a brain working alone at home the previous night. These thoughts raise the question about what takes place in school that makes it a uniquely schoolish place. My first uncluttered memory of school takes me back to the primary school classes at Saint Giles, where I had an oppressive crush on a school mistress whom I never forgave for getting pregnant and having to go tend her baby. I must have been five or six years of age. I demanded overwhelming constancy from that female teacher, my very special elementary school mistress. I thought she would always love only me, despite the fact that there were other suitors my age running after her. I learned poetry by thinking of her thin waist, encircled in a broad elastic belt clasped at the top of the billowing flowered skirt she loved to wear. Furthermore, seeking her constancy was surely more rewarding than running around with a dirty old blanket like Charlie Brown's Linus. However, my first connection to someone other than my parents took place in school. Saint Giles and all my schools after that were safe places that could inspire attachments of affection from time to time, despite the experiences of corporal punishment that I sometimes had to endure. Those who teach are capable of evoking peculiar emotional feelings in their charges.

Harrison College was an extension of Saint Giles in certain ways. I was older, thought more clearly, and also observed more carefully. I sought with more earnestness areas of competence and excellence. Playing basketball didn't make any sense to me. My height and size were reality-based discouragement. But my quickness and coordination led me to soccer, which has remained forever my favorite sport. Like any other youngster, I needed encouragement and support. I still remember the advice from my track coach at Harrison College, that my run-up to the high jump bar was too short and lengthening the run would improve my jump. Others told me I was holding on to the soccer ball too long and passing more quickly would enhance my effectiveness. There are numerous examples of occasions teachers encouraged me to try another way of solving a problem, making it clear they knew I would find the solution. I didn't see teachers always as being thoughtlessly cruel, not even in elementary school where the lickings were rife. I still can see my physical education teacher with his gentle hands as he helped a group of us boys learn to balance ourselves in a gymnastics performance that we put on at speech-day, with all the parents admiring us. He inspired us to put confidence in our bodies and trust our ability to maintain our balance. It was a wonderful lesson. He taught it without a trace of harshness.

One day, I took up a rock and threw it at an object floating in the wide canalized gutter that cut a path through the school grounds at

Harrison College. Someone obviously was witness to my hurling a projectile, and the result was a mandatory visit to the office of the headmaster, who was a British educator. The interview was short, and he quickly decided my punishment of two blows with a tamarind rod. He marched over to the area of his office where he kept several rods. He reached for one, pulled it out, and tested it by bending it with his hands, making sure that it had kept a certain flexibility. He ordered me to bend over, and his tamarind rod and my backside met each other with a coarse, unwelcome formality. The punishment was swift, limited, and effective. Throwing rocks at a schoolmate would have been punished more severely, so I was lucky. The message was clear. School was a safe place, and everybody conspired to expound that message in unmistakably lucid terms. This meant I had no appeals court to consult. I certainly did not run home to complain to my father, because I had no desire to run the risk of a second flogging, which would never have been as limited and precise as the first one.

As I say this, I recognize that these days many would consider the punishment brutal. But now that schools everywhere are producing shooting incidents and other surprises, I wonder if the views are changing. Of course, the other discordance between my days and these times is that we had obligatory morning prayers in elementary and secondary school. I know with certainty that the American view of separating prayers and school could never have my father's blessing. I cannot imagine not having heard the singing of the sixth-form boys, the older boys, and the intoning of the school's chaplain as he gave the final prayer on mornings at Harrison College. The chaplain sometimes played the piano that accompanied us, a task that often fell to other stalwarts in the sixth form. But I can still see the chaplain, with his habit of wearing a folded white handkerchief tucked around his parson's collar, raising his voice in prayer as only preachers can. How could anyone ask to remove that from a school? Elsewhere, perhaps, but not in Barbados.

In Barbados, I answered every teacher with the accompanying vocative of "Sir," and it was only after we moved to New York that I eventually got into the habit of addressing a teacher without that mark of respect. Still, I could never do what I saw a fellow student do the first day I was in summer class at a Manhattan school in 1956. The youngster entered the class late, while still remaining as relaxed as ever. Back

home in Barbados, I would have been trembling to be tardy, not knowing exactly what punishment awaited me. But this chap had no worries
at all, and then he said it: "Hi ya, teach." I was amazed at that student's
concentrated gall. That there could be such accepted horizontal democ-
racy in a high school was beyond my grasp at the time. I had never heard
such disrespect of teachers. I know that my father could never counte-
nance a mere child behaving as though he and the teacher were friends.
This is a cultural edict I've mentioned before, this thing of knowing who
your personal friends are. My father always took that very seriously, the
idea that children should know how to respect their elders and adults
who interacted with them regularly, like teachers and pastors.

It is a credit to my father's vision that he instinctively felt it necessary, even urgent, that his children receive the best education possible in
Barbados. Looking back, I think Harrison College, one of the premier
grammar schools of Barbados, is where I acquired my love of language
and honed my linguistic skills.

I once could recite several soliloquies from Shakespeare's plays, even
if in doing so I made my own changes to the text. Lack of precision in
the delivery did not alter my ownership of the Bard's words. Certain
familiar passages belonged to me, and I loved them with my own determined passion. There was a time I could amuse friends by reciting from
Macbeth every speech the three witches made, falsetto and all. I was not
restricted to English. I did limited justice to La Fontaine and recited his
fable about the two pilgrims struggling over their discovery of an oyster
on the beach. While they struggle about their find, Perrin Dandin
arrives to resolve the standoff. He eats the oyster and then gives to each
plaintiff an oyster shell, recommending that they both return home
peacefully.

This is not about showing off. It's about the love of language and
especially one's own tongue, about developing vocabulary, and seeing
the possibilities of turning a phrase, something I inherited from my
father. None of this affected my innate grasp of our beloved Bajan patois. Neither my father nor I ever thought it was useful to complain that
school instruction should be based on Ebonics. What difference would
that have made? There was still Sunday to contend with, and discourse
with others in the law courts, and communication in the international
cultural arena. And fundamentally closer to home, no one would have

convinced the Boss, and I could never have convinced my father, that it was all right not to be able to read the Bible lesson for a particular Sunday because the text was not written in Ebonics. I know Mamma always felt that language and hope were the same thing. That is why she stared me down the day I heard her call a stubborn young man a reprobate. I accused her of making up the word, and she calmly urged me to look the word up, not in a dictionary, but in her book, her Bible. I held my tongue before my arrogance got me into trouble with her. At any rate, the Ebonics argument did not gain ground in the Caribbean because of two practical points. First, because of the difference in accenting and in vocabulary, I did not understand the English-based patois spoken, for example, in Jamaica. Then I could barely follow the French-based patois of Dominica or Saint Lucia. So to focus on extending the influence of our Bajan patois at the expense of English was not a persuasive position. Even if we had no interest in communicating with the people up North or in Europe, we would still have to find a way to talk to our black brethren on the islands next door.

This does not mean that my own father did not claim the use of patois from time to time in his sermons. He did it in a way that brought his audience closer, just as he used it so often when holding court with his close friends. He also loved explicating his text on Sundays, going to the meaning of a Biblical term in Hebrew or in Greek so that he could get closer to what the early Christians meant by their peculiar turn of phrase. So he exhorted the knowledge of language as a tool to expand one's connection to people and the environment. Ebonics as a monolingual capacity was clearly too limiting. It cut off one's connections to others and diminished one's appreciation of the world.

With his experience, my father recognized that schools were there to impart knowledge that ultimately feeds our ego, makes us proud of ourselves, and helps define who we are. This was in addition to their basic role of providing technical information to us. One day while playing cricket in school, I shouted to a buddy that he had felt the ball well. I was complimenting him for having stopped the ball from continuing its run to the boundary. The games master turned around and seized the opportunity: To feel the cricket ball is not the same thing as to field the ball. Translated into the past tense, the ball was well fielded, not well felt. Feeling a ball is to palpate it. Now is the difference important? Of course it is, especially if teachers and parents have the vision that one day one's charges might be rubbing shoulders with the upper social, economic, and educational classes. But that requires vision, the capacity to see far and to hope strongly. I ultimately came to appreciate this Bajan approach, this tropical form of British seriousness, where the effort was made to create in us youngsters self-confidence melded with the grasp of what our black brains could accomplish. The linguistic honing was important insofar as it translated a symbolic sense of where we youngsters could conceivably be headed. Conversely, if one is headed nowhere, then much language isn't needed. At least, that's the way my father saw it.

School felt different once we got to Brooklyn, and the weather had its unique impact. There was not the Bajan proximity of classroom to the outdoors. Students did not wear uniforms to Brooklyn public schools. For the first time in my life, I saw teachers struggling with the problem of forcing students to leave their outer coats in their "homerooms" so as not to be able to leave school in the middle of the day. I had never heard of that problem back home. I could not imagine a boy my age taking off from school without the headmaster's permission and walking into town to window-shop. I suppose it existed, this business of cutting classes or skipping school. However, none of my friends participated in this practice in Barbados—certainly nobody who would have had to answer to a father like mine. I still learned a lot in this new American system, afforded through my encounters with Broadway theater, American history, economics, and my experiences with a highly structured and competitive American system of school sports.

The building of a youthful identity is not a matter of linear simplicity. Both in Barbados and in New York, it took a long time to meet a teacher who was excited by literary ideas that were relevant to things in my life. Despite the universality of Shakespeare, in Barbados we were not introduced to authors who opened a window on Caribbean life. I know it was a different time then. But we missed a lot. In addition, books were harder to obtain. I often would wait months before getting my hands on a particular Billy Bunter book, or one in the Western series about the gunslinger Sudden, or one of the Bulldog Drummond texts. The number of copies was limited, and there were many of us waiting for the reading pleasure afforded by these books.

In Brooklyn, access to books was easier, and I began to see the library as an extension of school. I went often after school, especially in winter, to the nearby branch library. A group of buddies and I usually took over a long, narrow table on which we did our homework. It was easier there than in small apartments, where academic and writing activity were generally conducted at the dining-room table. Students who tried to do their work in crowded homes like ours often came to school with telltale spots of grease on pages of their homework. I decided it was hard to complete homework in small apartments where large families were eating, watching television, talking business, planning next Sunday's Bible class, answering the telephone, and preparing for a host of other activities, all under the pressure of different work shifts.

I loved the quiet of the library, the easy accessibility of reference texts, the orderliness it forced on my thinking. It was a place where I learned to relax my neck and let my head fall back against a wall or the back of a chair. Then I could dream, roaming everywhere at will and changing the world so it was less pressingly painful. That's also the time I gathered up enough courage to talk to the beautiful Jamaican lass who ventured into the library every afternoon. We chatted in the muted and understated tones required by libraries. The requisite brevity of the conversation suited my youth, my inexperience, and my personality.

The other striking thing about libraries, which was helpful to me in this new American culture that was so disorienting to new arrivals, was how it enhanced evenness and equality. All the macho traits were left at the door. Silence was golden. Prancing up and down was discouraged. There was no place for gang members to be threatening, not in a library. So a part of that library near my school became my space, shared only with a group of other boys who held on to the values people like our fathers had inculcated in us.

My mentioning values again leads me back to the business of how much time I spent in church on Sundays in Barbados. Looking back, I comment repetitiously that life has changed significantly since the years when every Sunday morning took me to the 9:30 Sunday school at the Moravian church on Roebuck Street. I went there on my trusted bicycle, and I must say I loved it. I never cease to marvel at the commitment of the teachers who ran that school, who took us in without ever caring one whit about where we came from or what the religion of our parents was. We had discussions about all the major Bible stories and just learned how to treat everybody with fundamental respect. The teachers told us about the Bible and Christian principles and got us talking and reading and thinking. Nobody ever expected us to become Moravians. In fact, at first I did not realize that when my father occasionally took me with him to visit the pastor at Mount Tabor Church, he was actually taking me to see the individual who was in charge of a branch of the Moravian Church. Mount Tabor was a sedate oasis in my mind, where people were friendly and warm toward children, who could run and jump and make noise because of the beautiful seclusion of the place. I never linked any of it to the Moravians. I just saw them as behaving toward me with spectacular warmth, understanding, and a type of admiration that would please a child.

When it was time to be confirmed, to make an informed choice about becoming a member of a particular Protestant denomination, I became an Anglican. The decision was taken without any formal reflection or discussion around the dining table, and without considering the inconveniences and advantages of becoming an Anglican. Both my father and Mamma had families with strong ties to the Anglicans. So the decision never seemed bizarre or unusual to me. And confirmation at the hands of the bishop eventually came as a natural step in the evolution of things, although I continued to frequent other churches. My father encouraged multiple memberships in churches. He lived out that idea by preaching wherever he was invited.

While I sang in the choir of an Anglican Church, I also attended afternoon Sunday school with the Methodists. And I had been to services at the Christian Mission in Bank Hall, Brother Tucker's church in lower Station Hill, and at the Nazarene Church in Welches. I certainly had the greatest familiarity with the Anglican form of service, and I knew by heart many of their prayers and other rituals. I had no particular objection to choosing the Anglicans as my home base. It coincided smoothly with my membership in the Cathedral Choir, which meant that I sang at Sunday morning matins, Sunday evensong, and at the midweek evening service on Wednesdays at half past seven. On the last Sunday of every month, I also sang at an 8 a.m. communion service. In addition to all that, the choirboys attended practice three times a week. With that much singing, it is easy to understand how I managed to learn many of the psalms, hymns, prayers, and even anthems by heart.

I had always hoped that church ritual was immutable and only subject to change decreed by me. There is, no doubt, something provincial
and self-centered about this view. I had come to expect that having
acquired a distinct taste for the rituals, having spe would prepare me for
certain unique circumstances. For example, if I ever became very sick,
I could follow certain prayers even if I couldn't read them. I also always
remembered the event of my father's having undergone surgery. The
operation was completed, and he was coming out of the anesthesia. In
this semiconscious state, said the surgeon, my father started reciting
one of the communion prayers about not approaching the communion
table trusting in his own worthiness but in the grace of God. It had an
impact on this doctor, and my father took it as a sign of his being at
peace with the surgery because of his faith. I saw it as an indication of
the utility of maintaining a ritual intact.

As a part of this discussion with my father, I liked to draw his attention to the simple business of the call and response we both knew so
well. The priest would say, "The Lord be with you." Then the congregation would respond, "And with thy spirit." Now the congregation is
responding, "And also with you." I have been more severe than my
father in assessing the wisdom of such a change. And to crown it all,
they took away my beloved King James Version of the Bible and started reading all kinds of modernized translations. My father did not see
the modern texts as anathema. He would use them at times, although
he often reverted to the King James Version to make a comparison. I
did not understand how anybody could be tempted to memorize verses of the modern style.

I have been attending a church where the prayers and other parts
usually sung by the priest are now said by him or by someone else. This
has been especially problematic for me. I remember when my father
would switch into high gear and intone, "... Therefore with angels and
archangels, and with all the company of heaven, we laud and magnify
thy glorious name, evermore praising thee and saying ..." in the communion service, just before the choir would move into "Holy, holy,
holy ..." I have found it hard to accept that some priests are now avoiding singing their part. Nobody asked my opinion about this. But, to
me, these changes spell no progress at all. How can the powers that be,
those in charge, make changes that essentially eradicate the memories
that hold my father and me together? It represents an assault on my past,

a way of claiming that what we had together didn't really exist or it wasn't important. I cannot give in to these onslaughts. I holding strain. Man, I holding strain fuh so.

ABOUT THE AUTHOR

Ezra Griffith is a Professor of Psychiatry and of African-American Studies at Yale University, New Haven, Connecticut. For many years, he has taught courses that focus on the task of telling stories about black lives throughout the Diaspora. In collaboration with colleagues, he edited: *Clinical Guidelines in Cross-Cultural Mental Health*; and *Racial and Ethnic Identity: Psychological Development and Creative Expression*. He recently authored *Race and Excellence: My Dialogue with Chester Pierce*, which recounts the life and accomplishments of renowned Harvard intellectual, Professor Chester Pierce.

Breinigsville, PA USA
30 October 2009
226745BV00002B/2/A